Little Pebble™

All Kinds of Weather

Rainy Weather
A 4D BOOK

by Sally Lee

D1404527

PEBBLE
a capstone imprint

Download the Capstone app!

- Ask an adult to download the Capstone 4D app.

- Scan the cover and stars inside the book for additional content.

When you scan a spread, you'll find fun extra stuff to go with this book! You can also find these things on the web at www.capstone4D.com using the password: rainy.01846

Little Pebble is published by Pebble
1710 Roe Crest Drive, North Mankato,
Minnesota 56003
www.mycapstone.com

Library of Congress Cataloging-in-Publication Data
is available on the Library of Congress website.

ISBN 978-1-9771-0184-6 (library binding)
ISBN 978-1-9771-0191-4 (paperback)
ISBN 978-1-9771-0197-6 (ebook pdf)

Editorial Credits
Marissa Kirkman, editor; Bobbie Nuytten, designer; Tracy Cummins, media researcher; Kris Wilfahrt, production specialist

Photo Credits
iStockphoto: AfricaImages, 9; Shutterstock: A3pfamily, 1, andreiuc88, 5, Evgeny Atamanenko, Cover, Gts, 13, irin-k, 17, KENG MERRY Paper Art, Design Element, Love Silhouette, 19, Maria Sbytova, 21, ND700, 15, scsphtgrph, 7, MarynaG, 11.

Printed and bound in the United States.
PA021

Table of Contents

Drip Drop

Gray clouds fill the sky.

Rain falls from the clouds.

The ground is wet.

It is rainy today!

We Need Rain

All living things need water.
Rain brings water for
plants and animals.

Rain gives us
water to drink.
We wash in it.
We play in it.

What Makes Rain?

The sun's rays heat water.

The water evaporates.

Puddles disappear.

The water becomes vapor.

The air is cold up high.

The water vapor turns

into tiny drops.

We see them as clouds.

Tiny water drops join together.

They get heavy.

The bigger drops fall

to earth as rain.

Clouds help forecast
the weather.
White puffy clouds mean
no rain.

Low gray clouds bring rain.

Dark clouds can bring storms.

Have Fun!

Put on your rain boots.

Jump in puddles.

Splash!

Glossary

cloud—a white or gray mass of water droplets and dust in the air; raindrops form in certain types of clouds

evaporate—to turn from a liquid into a gas

forecast—a report of future weather conditions

puddle—a small pool of water; puddles often collect on the ground after it rains

ray—a line of light that beams out from something bright

storm—bad weather; there can be strong winds, rain, or snow, and sometimes thunder and lightning in a storm

vapor—a gas made from a liquid

Read More

Hansen, Grace. *Rain*. Weather. Minneapolis: Abdo Kids, 2016.

Olien, Rebecca. *The Water Cycle at Work*. Water in Our World. North Mankato, Minn.: Capstone Press, 2016.

Rustad, Martha E. H. *Today Is a Rainy Day*. What Is the Weather Today? North Mankato, Minn.: Capstone Press, 2017.

Internet Sites

Use FactHound to find Internet sites related to this book.

Visit www.facthound.com

Just type in 9781977101846 and go.

Check out projects, games and lots more at
www.capstonekids.com

Critical Thinking Questions

1. How do we use the water that rain brings for us?

2. What happens to water when it evaporates?

3. What kind of weather is on its way when you see dark clouds?

Index

CRITICAL ACCLAIM FOR ROBERT B. PARKER

'Parker writes old-time, stripped-to-the-bone, hard-boiled school of Chandler... His novels are funny, smart and highly entertaining... There's no writer I'd rather take on an aeroplane'
– *Sunday Telegraph*

'Parker packs more meaning into a whispered "yeah" than most writers can pack into a page'
– *Sunday Times*

'Why Robert Parker's not better known in Britain is a mystery. His best series featuring Boston-based PI Spenser is a triumph of style and substance'
– *Daily Mirror*

'Robert B. Parker is one of the greats of the American hard-boiled genre'
– *Guardian*

'Nobody does it better than Parker...'
– *Sunday Times*

'Parker's sentences flow with as much wit, grace and assurance as ever, and Stone is a complex and consistently interesting new protagonist'
– *Newsday*

'If Robert B. Parker doesn't blow it, in the new series he set up in *Night Passage* and continues with *Trouble in Paradise*, he could go places and take the kind of risks that wouldn't be seemly in his popular Spenser stories'
– **Marilyn Stasio,** *New York Times*

THE SPENSER NOVELS

THE JESSE STONE MYSTERIES

THE SUNNY RANDALL MYSTERIES

ALSO BY ROBERT B. PARKER

*Available from No Exit Press

ROBERT B. PARKER

MELANCHOLY BABY

A SUNNY RANDALL MYSTERY

NO EXIT PRESS

This edition published 2015

First published in the UK in 2005
by No Exit Press,
an imprint of Oldcastle Books
PO Box 394, Harpenden,
Herts, AL5 1XJ, UK

A CIP catalogue record for this book is available from the British Library.

ISBN
978-1-84344-438-1 (print)
978-1-84344-318-6 (epub)
978-1-84344-319-3 (kindle)
978-1-84344-320-9 (pdf)

2 4 6 8 10 9 7 5 3

Typeset in 11.25pt Minion
by Avocet Typeset, Somerton, Somerset

Printed in Great Britain by Clays Ltd, St Ives plc

For Jean:
Like the kicker in a mint julep for two

1

My ex-husband was getting married to a woman I wanted to kill. I didn't actually know her, and killing her would only make matters worse. But I got as much pleasure out of the idea as I could before I had to let go of it.

He didn't take the coward's way out and simply send me an invitation. He came to see me.

'She better be nice to Rosie,' I said.

'I wouldn't let anyone not be nice to Rosie,' Richie said. 'Do you think I love Rosie less than you do?'

I didn't say anything for a bit, then, finally, I said, 'No.'

'Thank you,' Richie said.

'And, obviously, stupid question, you love this woman?'

'Yes,' Richie said.

It got out before I could shut it off.

'More than you love me?' I said.

He didn't say anything for a bit, then, finally, he said, 'No.'

'This raises a question,' I said.

'It is, I've found, possible to love more than one person,' Richie said. 'I love you, and I love her. She's willing to marry me.'

'And you want to be married?' I said.

'Yes.'

'And I don't.'

'I know.'

'It has nothing to do with not loving you,' I said.

'I know.'

'I just can't be married, Richie.'

'I know.'

I had been looking at Richie for so long. He got a dark shadow on his face if he didn't shave every day. He had the strongest-looking hands I'd ever seen. He had thick black hair and wore it short. He seemed never to need a haircut. I knew what he looked like naked. I knew what he looked like asleep. I knew what he smelled like and sounded like and felt like. I knew how he thought and what he thought.

Richie stood.

'I wish there was something else to say, Sunny.'

I stood, too. He opened his arms. We hugged each other. It was eviscerating. Richie stepped away; neither of us spoke. He bent over and picked up Rosie and kissed her on the nose. And hugged her. Then he put her back down and turned and left.

I sat on my bed for a time. My eyes filled but I didn't cry. Rosie jumped up beside me and lay down and wagged her tail.

'Don't you ever, ever love her,' I said to Rosie.

Rosie looked at me as only bull terriers can look. She offered no objection. I wiped my eyes and walked down the length of my loft to the kitchen and got a bottle of Irish whiskey and poured some in a highball glass. I took it with me to the kitchen table and sat in my chair and looked out the window. Rosie came and got up in her chair and looked hopeful. I took a cracker out of the canister on the table and gave it to her. My sister, Elizabeth, would love this. My father would ask if there was anything he could do to help. My mother would assume it was my fault.

I drank a little more whiskey. I could feel a real cry beginning to form in my throat. I tried to swallow it. But then I was taking little short breaths, and making little short sounds, and it was too late. I gave up and let it come. Rosie looked at me uncertainly. She wasn't used to this. I cried hard for a while, leaning my forehead against my left hand. With my right I tried to comfort Rosie, who was nervous.

We'd been divorced for five years. What the hell did I expect? It wasn't like he'd been celibate all that time, or I had. It wasn't just the finality of my former husband remarrying. It wasn't even that I loved him still, though I did. It was the unyielding reality that, as far as I could tell, I couldn't marry anybody, live with anybody, share my life fully with anybody.

I drank some more whiskey.

I listened to the paroxysmal quality of my own crying.

I bent over and picked up Rosie and held her in my lap.

'Only you,' I said to her. 'You're the only one I can live with.'

I rocked back and forth in my chair with her for a time.

'Only you.' I gasped. 'Only you. Only you.'

Why can't I live with anyone but a dog?

What the fuck is wrong with me?

2

In the morning I was still red-eyed, even after I showered and put on makeup. By muscle memory, I fed Rosie and took her out. When I came in with her, I wasn't hungry. I drank some orange juice and made some coffee. The phone rang. When I answered it, my voice sounded thick.

'Sunny?'

'Yes.'

'It's Barbara Stein. Do you have a cold?'

I said, 'Yes.' It seemed more dignified than, 'No, I've been crying a lot.'

'Oh, I'm sorry. Are you well enough to do a little detective work?'

'Yes.'

'You're still in the detective business?'

'Yes.'

'Oh, good. I have a young woman who came into my office late yesterday. I'd done legal work for her family from time to time. You know, closings, wills, that kind of thing. She wants to find her biological parents.'

'Can't you help her with that?'

'We're a small firm,' Barbara said. 'Just me and Jake and a paralegal… and this is going to be a little tricky, I think. The parents claim she's theirs, that she's not adopted.'

'DNA?'

'The parents won't submit. Say it's an insulting invasion of their privacy.'

'Oh, my,' I said. 'Birth records?'

'So far,' Barbara said, 'we can't locate any.'

'What makes her think she is adopted?'

'She won't say. Can you meet with her?'

'I suppose,' I said.

'Can you come to my office?'

'You still in Andover?' I said.

She was. We made a date and I hung up. What I didn't feel like doing was working. But maybe, in the long run, it was better for me than sitting by the window, drinking Irish whiskey. Rosie went to the coat rack by the door and stared at her leash. I didn't feel like walking her, either. Actually, I didn't feel like doing anything. Maybe talking to someone. Usually when I felt this bad, and I had never felt this bad since Richie and I divorced, I talked to Richie. My mother and my sister were out. My best friend, Julie, would genuinely care, but she would have a little inside, unspoken thrill of satisfaction that my love life was fucked up, too. And I would sense it, and it would make me mad. My father would hug me. But what could he say?

'We're awful goddamned alone,' I said to Rosie.

She continued to gaze at her leash.

'Except for Spike,' I said.

Rosie's gaze toward the leash wavered for a moment when she heard Spike's name. She loved Spike almost as much as she loved me… and Richie. And she always had fun with him. I tried to smile at her.

'Okay,' I said.

My voice still sounded hoarse to me, and thick with sadness.

'We will kill two birds. You'll get your walk, and Spike will make me feel better. Maybe.'

3

Rosie had on her black-and-white leash, which matched her black-and-white collar, which matched her coloration. She pranced, and I walked along Atlantic Avenue through the maelstrom of Big Dig construction to Spike's Place on Marshall Street, near Quincy Market. Spike used to manage it when it was a casual restaurant during the day, and perform in it when it was a comedy club at night. Now he owned it. The first thing he had done was change the name to Spike's Place. The second thing he'd done was to retire from show business. He canceled the comedy club and upgraded the dinner menu.

The décor was still the bare-beams and weathered-brick look it always had been. But the food was greatly improved. The service was good. The help dressed better. And Spike, now with a financial stake in things, had attempted an attitude upgrade, which, given his temperament, was not entirely successful.

Inside the front door of Spike's Place was the hostess stand, and on the table was a small sign that read *No dogs allowed, except seeing-eye.* The hostess, a pretty young woman in a yellow linen dress, knew me, knew Rosie, and made no comment as she led us to a banquette for two along the wall at a right angle to the bar. Rosie hopped up beside me on the banquette.

'You want to see Spike?' the hostess said.

'Please,' I said.

'I'll tell him you're here,' the hostess said. 'You want anything?'

'Just some coffee,' I said.

'I'll send some over,' the hostess said.

She spoke to a waitress as she walked toward the back of the room. The four women at the next table were having an early lunch and discussing a recent production at the American Repertory Theatre. They seemed enthusiastic. The waitress brought me coffee and a roll.

'Roll's for Rosie,' the waitress said.

'Thank you.'

I stirred some milk and Splenda into my coffee. Rosie fixed a beady, laser-like stare on the roll. I broke off a small piece and put it on the table in front of her, and she ate it.

A mature woman with harlequin eyeglasses gazed at us in horror.

'That's offensive,' she said.

I leaned my head back against the banquette and closed my eyes and took in some air, and said nothing. When I opened my eyes, Spike was standing in front of my table. He was a very big bear of a man, in all senses. His hair was short and his shirt was crisp white and his tan slacks had a sharp crease. He wore mahogany loafers with no socks. The loafers had a high shine. He was looking at me hard. Then he pulled a chair away from another table and sat down across from me.

'What's wrong?' he said.

The mature woman gestured to the hostess, who walked over.

'I'd like to speak with the manager, please,' she said.

The hostess was charmed.

'That would be me,' she said. 'I'm Miranda.'

'Well, are you going to do anything about this dog?'

'Well, Rosie is sort of a regular patron,' Miranda said.

'Which I gather means you do not plan to intervene?'

'Perhaps a happy compromise,' Miranda said, 'would be to offer you a different table.'

'I prefer to sit where I am,' the lady said. 'And I wish to speak with your superior.'

'You certainly may,' Miranda said. 'The owner is sitting right next to you. Spike himself.'

The mature woman and her three mature companions all spoke as if they had taken elocution lessons at Radcliffe. And they looked as if they shopped at an Ellen Tracy discount store.

'How do you do?' the mature woman said.

'How do you do?' Spike said.

'I'm sorry to bother you, but I saw your sign when I came in.

It says *No dogs allowed, except seeing-eye.'*

Spike looked at Rosie, and then at Miranda, then back at the woman.

'Oh, of course, ma'am. I see your point completely.'

He stood up.

'I'll take care of it right away.'

Spike walked to the hostess stand and reached behind it and opened the drawer. All of his movements were as graceful and precise as if he weighed half of what he weighed. He took a black felt-tipped Magic Marker from the drawer, bent over, and carefully, after the part that said *except seeing-eye,* wrote in a neat hand: *and Rosie Randall.* Then he put the Magic Marker back in the drawer, stepped back, and looked at the sign. Nodded with satisfaction, and returned to his chair.

'Thanks for caring,' he said to the lady in the harlequin glasses.

'But you... you... you can't just change the sign and allow dogs to eat off the table in a restaurant.'

Spike looked at them, puzzled for a moment. I knew he was struggling with his attitude adjustment.

'Perhaps if Miranda got you a better table?' Spike said.

'It's not a question of a better table,' the mature woman said. 'It's a question, if I may say so, of hygiene.'

The adjustment was sliding.

'Rosie's had all her shots,' Spike said. 'I don't think you'll infect her.'

Miranda had been hovering near, knowing how tenuous Spike's hold on civility was.

'Ladies, if you'll come with me,' Miranda said. 'There's a lovely table by the window. I'll have your server move everything... and lunch will be on me.'

It was a chance to finish lunch, preserve their dignity, and save a few bucks. They took it. In maybe a minute they were reseated, their plates were transferred, and they were eating again, though all of them glared occasionally at me and Rosie and Spike.

'Never fire Miranda,' I said to Spike.

'God no,' he said. 'I'd put myself out of business in a month.'

We were quiet. Spike looked at me. Then he got up and came around and sat on the banquette beside me.

'Something bad is bothering you,' he said. 'And I want to know what.'

4

I started to tear up again as I told him, and when I got through, he put his arms around me and pulled me against him. This made Rosie vaguely uneasy, until he scooped her in, too, and the three of us sat in close embrace while I cried a little.

After a while I stopped, and with my face still against his chest said, 'I don't know what to do.'

'Of course you don't,' Spike said.

'I know we were divorced,' I said. 'I know he slept with other people and God knows I did, too.'

'But sometimes you slept with each other,' Spike said softly, 'even though you were divorced, and you still loved him, and you were pretty sure he loved you, and you sort of knew that someday it would work out, and you'd be together again, in some way or other.'

I nodded against his chest. It was like snuggling a sandbag.

'And now the sonovabitch is getting married and you can't think that anymore.'

I nodded again.

'Even though you divorced him originally.'

'Yes.'

My voice sounded small and muffled against him. He didn't say anything else, just kept his arm around me and patted my back gently. With his other hand, he gave Rosie a piece of her dinner roll. I got my breathing under control after a while, and he let me go and I sat up straight. Spike handed me a napkin and I blotted my eyes dry, trying not to make too much of a mess of my makeup.

'For what it's worth,' Spike said, 'this is as bad as it's going to get. In a while it will get better.'

'It doesn't feel that way.'

'It will get better,' Spike said.

'What the hell is wrong with me?' I said. 'I can't live with him, but when he finds somebody that can, I have a breakdown.'

'Because the first time you left him. Now he's leaving you.'

'You think I'm that childish?'

'Sure,' Spike said.

'I can't live with anyone,' I said.

'I know.'

'But why can't I?'

'I don't know.'

Rosie had settled in comfortably between us now that there was no more hugging and crying, and kept her eyes on the roll. Spike broke off another small piece and fed it to her.

'I don't know, either,' I said. 'That's the awful thing.'

'Weren't you seeing a shrink a while ago?'

'Dr Copeland, yes, but that was business. I was consulting on that Melissa Joan Hall thing.'

'But didn't you go see him for a while afterwards?'

'Just a couple of times,' I said. 'I didn't see any reason to go really.'

''Cause Richie wasn't getting married, and neither were you, so you and he could be whatever you and he were.'

I nodded.

'And, as I recall, you were bopping that guy from LA.'

'Spike!'

'Which made it easier to feel like you were happy,' Spike said. 'Right now you feel badly alone.'

'Except for you,' I said.

'And as we both know, I'm gayer than three humming birds,' Spike said.

'Doesn't mean I don't love you,' I said.

'Doesn't mean I don't love you, either. But that's not what we're talking about.'

'What are we talking about?'

'You need to see a shrink.'

'Oh, God,' I said.

'We need to know what's wrong with you.' He grinned at me. 'I can only take you so far.'

'That seems so long a hill to climb.'

Spike nodded.

'I mean, do you think I'm crazy?'

'I think you need to know what's making you unhappy.'

'Duh,' I said. 'Richie's marriage might have something to do with it.'

'I think you need to know why that's making you so unhappy.'

'Because I love him, for crissake.'

'Then I think you need to know why you love him and can't live with him.'

I was silent. Spike gave Rosie the final bite of roll. The ladies that Rosie had offended finished their free lunches and got up and left. They were careful not to notice me or Rosie.

'You bastard,' I said to Spike.

He smiled.

'Explain to me where I'm wrong,' he said.

'You're not wrong. It's why I called you a bastard.'

5

Barbara Stein had a law office on the second floor of the old Musgrove Building in downtown Andover, with a nice view of the town library. There was an outer office for her paralegal, two small offices for her and her husband, Jake Kaplan, and a modest conference room. Barbara, her client, and I were in the conference room.

The client's name was Sarah Markham. She looked about twenty. She was taller than I was, and slim, with long, straight, dark hair, large brown eyes, and a lot of dark makeup. She wore low-slung pants and a cropped long-sleeved T-shirt that exposed her navel. She had rings on most of her fingers, including one on her left thumb, and her nails were painted black. It was a hideous fashion, and thankfully, I was just old enough that it was not required. Barbara had gray hair pulled back into a tight knot, and round, black-rimmed eyeglasses. Exposed navels were not an issue with her.

'I don't look like anyone in my family,' Sarah told me.

'Eye color?' I said.

I had a dim sense, lingering from my science-requirement biology class, that two blue-eyed parents couldn't produce a brown-eyed child.

'Except that,' she said. 'But I don't look anything like them.'

'What do your parents say?'

'They say I'm their biological child.'

'Barbara tells me they won't allow DNA testing.'

'No,' Sarah said, 'they won't.'

'Because it's demeaning?'

'Yes. They're pretty phobic about doctors and things.'

'Things?' I said.

I was trying to focus. Trying to care about her problem.

'I think my mother has a religious thing about it.'

'About DNA testing.'

'I guess,' Sarah said. 'They're pretty phobic, you know?'

'Give me an example,' I said.

'Oh, I don't know. They're scared of everything?'

'Besides doctors and God, who are they scared of?' I said.

'Everyone,' she said. 'What difference does it make? How is that helping me find my birth parents?'

Vague and impatient. What a lovely combination.

'They are not at ease with me,' Barbara said.

'Tell me again, how did Sarah get to you?' I said.

'I have done some general legal work for her family,' Barbara said.

'Have they always been ill at ease with you?'

'No, it's more since I've been helping Sarah.'

'For God's sake,' Sarah said. 'You're supposed to be a detective? Why don't you detect something instead of asking all these dumb questions?'

'Asking a lot of dumb questions is sort of how you do that,' I said. 'How old are you?'

'Twenty-one.'

'Live at home?'

'I'm in college. I live in the dorm. I'm at home during vacations.'

'Where do you go?'

'I'm going into my senior year at Taft University,' Sarah said. 'What difference does all that make?'

'I don't know,' I said. 'How will you pay my fee?'

'I have money from my grandfather.'

'Does he give it to you, or did you inherit?'

'He left me a trust fund, he started it when I was born.'

'Did you know your grandfather?'

'I don't remember him.'

'Paternal or maternal?' I said.

'Excuse me?'

'Which of your parents did he father?' I said.

'He was my mother's father.'

'Was he wealthy?'

Sarah gave me an it's-none-of-your-business look. I bore up under it.

'I don't know. He didn't put so much in to start, but... have you heard of compound interest?'

'Only secondhand,' I said. 'Can your parents control the fund?'

'Not now.'

'The money passed outright to Sarah,' Barbara said. 'When she turned eighteen.'

'Besides appearance,' I said, 'is there anything else that makes you think you're not biologically related?'

Sarah breathed in deeply and looked even more annoyed, but she answered me.

'There's a ton of clues,' she said. 'They were always talking when I was little about how my mother couldn't have kids... *except of course you, Sarah.* It was like they'd catch themselves.'

I nodded.

'What else?'

'They can't find my birth certificate,' she said. 'They don't remember which hospital I was born in.'

'Where were you born?'

'Chicago, Illinois.'

'When did you move?'

'I don't know. It was when I was a baby.'

'So what's your earliest memory of where you lived?'

'Here.'

'Andover,' I said.

'Yes,' she answered, in a tone that suggested that I was very stupid. 'Isn't that what I just said?'

'What you said was "here." I was confirming that you meant Andover, and not simply Massachusetts.'

'Oh, for heaven's sake,' Sarah said. 'Do you want the job or not?'

'Sarah,' I said. 'I know how to do this, and you do not. But I have to do it the way I know how. And I have to be able to stand the client. So far, I can't.'

Sarah looked at me in astonishment and began to cry. Perfect. Maybe I could join her and we could both have a good cry and fall into each other's arms. Barbara got up and patted Sarah's shoulder.

'Sunny Randall is a very good detective. I know she can help you, but she has to ask questions. I know it seems clear to you. But Sunny's just come aboard.'

Sarah sniffled and nodded. And sniffled and wiped her eyes and blew her nose on a Kleenex that Barbara gave her.

'Yes. Please. I'm sorry. I'll tell you anything you need to know.'

'With less attitude?' I said. 'I've not been having the best week of my life, either.'

'I'm sorry. I didn't realize. I didn't mean to have attitude. Really, I'll try to tell you everything.'

'That'll be good,' I said. 'Can you get me pictures of yourself, and of your mother and father?'

I knew she wanted to ask me why. And she knew it would annoy me. We looked at each other.

19

'It will help with the question of identity,' I said.

She shrugged.

'Sure,' she said.

'Good,' I said. 'Shall we discuss my fee?'

6

Dr Copeland was still a large, athletic-looking shrink. He was wearing a brown tweed jacket today, with a white Oxford shirt and maroon knit tie. His dark hair was still slicked straight back. He still wore big, round, black-rimmed glasses. He was still immaculate.

When I was seated across the desk from him in his office, he said, 'It's nice to see you again, Sunny.'

I felt sort of thrilled. He called me by my first name.

'Yes,' I said. 'I'm glad to see you, too.'

I did not venture to call him Max. He smiled and sat back.

'Richie is getting married,' I said.

He nodded.

'You remember Richie?' I said.

'Your former husband,' Copeland said.

'Yes. Do you remember everything we talked about?'

'If I don't, I'll ask you to remind me,' Copeland said.

'Last time we talked, you said the bond between us was powerful, or something like that.'

'I remember,' he said.

'What do you think now?' I said.

'I also said I didn't know where it would lead,' Copeland said.

'Covered yourself,' I said.

Copeland didn't say anything.

'I guess I'm mad at you,' I said.

Copeland nodded.

'The hell of it is,' I said, 'you were right. There is a strong bond between us.'

Copeland nodded.

'But I can't live with him. I can't live with anybody, really. And… Richie's too… too traditional, I guess. He wants a wife and probably children.'

Copeland was leaning forward. He had his fingertips together in front of him and, with his elbows resting on the arms of his chair, he tapped his steepled forefingers against his chin softly as he listened.

'I'm thirty-seven,' I said. 'If I'm going to have kids, I better do it now.'

Copeland smiled.

'You have a few years,' he said.

'It doesn't matter. I couldn't be a wife and mother anyway.'

Copeland nodded just as if it were perfectly normal for a woman to reject marriage and children.

'I don't know anyone like me,' I said.

'That doesn't wish marriage and children?'

'Yes.'

'Believe me,' Copeland said. 'There are many.'

'I don't know what to do,' I said.

'What would you like to do?' Copeland said.

'I'd like to stop feeling like I've been shot in the stomach,' I said.

'I would think that some member of the Boston psychotherapy community could help you with that,' Copeland said.

'I want you to help me.'

He shook his head.

'Why not?' I said.

'I would like to work with you, Sunny, but I am retiring.'

'You're not old enough to retire,' I said.

He nodded as if to acknowledge a compliment.

'I'm finishing up with my current patients and will be closing the office before the end of the year.'

I felt panicky.

'You too,' I said.

'Another rejection?' he said.

'I screwed up my courage and screwed up my courage to

21

finally come here, and you are going to retire.'

'It is, of course, not personal,' Copeland said.

'Not to you,' I said.

'Well,' Copeland said, 'in a sense it is. I am, after all, the one who's retiring.'

'I know,' I said. 'I know.'

'I can refer you to someone.'

'Like who?'

'I need to make some phone calls,' Copeland said. 'To see who is currently taking new patients.'

'I was counting on you,' I said.

'I know. I'm sorry. But I can assure you that I will refer you to someone smart enough and' – he smiled a little – 'tough enough to help you with this.'

'And you think I can be helped?'

'I'm sure,' Copeland said. 'Generally, as you probably understand, what one needs in successful therapy is a good shrink, and a patient with the courage and brains to work on the issue. I can provide the good shrink. I know you have the rest.'

I felt short of breath, but I also felt reassured. I breathed in some air and let it out. I did that a couple times.

Then I said, 'One request.'

Copeland bowed his head in a small encouraging gesture.

'Not Dr Melvin,' I said.

'No,' Copeland said. 'Not Dr Melvin.'

7

Sarah's parents lived on School Street, which branched off from Main Street opposite the Academy. Their house was down the hill a ways. It was a very large, white nineteenth-century house with a wide wraparound porch. Classes had started at Taft, and Sarah would be gone. It seemed as good a time as any to go visit her parents. It had to be done sometime.

Her mother answered my ring. She was a small, dark-haired woman with a furtive manner. She looked about fifty.

'Hi,' I said. 'I'm Sunny Randall.'

'Oh, Ms Randall, thank you, please come in.'

The house was big and cluttered and full of costly furniture that didn't go together very well. Mrs Markham scuttled ahead of me, as if she was afraid someone would yell at her.

'Please, let's go in the sunroom,' she said. 'I hope you won't find it too warm there.'

'I'm sure it will be fine,' I said.

'George,' Mrs Markham called. 'Sunny Randall is here.'

George was on his feet when we went into the sunroom.

'Miss Randall,' he said. 'Thanks for coming.'

He was tall enough, with a lot of bushy hair, wearing the kind of low-cut reading glasses you can buy at the drugstore. And he had the same stoop-shouldered bearing his wife had. They both looked as if they expected a scolding.

'Thanks for seeing me,' I said.

'Oh, no, no,' he said. 'Our pleasure, really.'

He had a deep, hearty voice with very little accent. The boom of it was at odds with his tentative bearing.

'Will you have coffee?' Mrs Markham said.

'No, thank you.'

'Or some tea?'

'No,' I said. 'Thanks.'

'Spring water?'

I smiled and shook my head.

'I think we have some V8 juice,' she said.

Jesus Christ!

'Nothing, thank you,' I said. 'You understand that I am here as your daughter's representative.'

'Oh, yes,' Mrs Markham said.

I looked at Mister.

'Yes,' he said. 'Certainly.'

'She has employed me to locate her birth parents.'

They both smiled and nodded.

'What can you tell me about that?' I said.

23

Mister and Missus looked at each other.

'Oh, my, I'm sorry,' George said. 'But we really don't know what to say.'

'Because?'

'Well, I...' he looked at his wife. 'We... I don't wish to be offensive. But we are her birth parents.'

'She doesn't think so.'

'I know. We feel so sad about that. We've told her and told her.'

Mrs Markham chimed in. 'We have, we've told her, and she still doesn't believe us. What can we do?'

'Allow your DNA to be tested.'

Neither of them said anything.

'Sarah tells me that you've declined to do that.'

'We just, we... it isn't something we can do,' Mrs Markham said. 'Is it, George?'

'No, we can't do that.'

'Why not?' I said.

Neither of them said anything. Both of them looked at the floor. I waited. The air was thick with silence. Both of them kept shaking their heads.

'Are you uncomfortable with your daughter feeling she's adopted, when in fact she isn't?'

They both nodded.

'Wouldn't DNA testing make all this go away?'

Neither of them appeared to hear me.

'Or if she were adopted, what would be so bad about that?' I said.

'She's not adopted,' Mrs Markham said to the floor.

'Then why not undergo a simple procedure to prove it?'

Nothing.

'Sarah tells me she was born in Chicago and moved here to Andover as an infant.'

'Yes,' Mrs Markham said.

'When would that have been?'

Mrs Markham looked at Mr Markham and he looked back. They both frowned thoughtfully.

Then Mrs Markham said, '1982. The fall of 1982.'

I smiled charmingly and said, 'Why did you move?'

'We didn't want our daughter raised in the city.'

'We wanted a more exclusive environment for her,' Mr Markham said.

'Why here?'

'We hoped perhaps she could go to the Academy when she got older.'

'Did she?'

'No.'

'The best-laid plans,' I said.

'Excuse me?' Mrs Markham said.

'I was being literary,' I said.

'Oh.'

'Any other reason for moving here?'

'We had friends, I think.' She smiled at me so I wouldn't be mad. 'It's so long ago, but I think some friends had lived here and said it was nice.'

'Good, solid New England values,' Mr Markham said.

People said things like that – *it was so long ago*. But in fact twenty-one years isn't so long ago. Most people can remember most things of any importance from twenty-one years ago. Twenty-one years ago, after a high-school dance, I was making out in the back of a car with Bruce McBride and trying to decide how far to let him go. I was wearing a blue spaghetti strap dress, and high heels that made walking difficult. My mother thought the outfit looked cheap, but my father had said if I was old enough to have a date, I was old enough to decide how I wanted to look.

'Probably can't remember their name,' I said.

'No, I'm so sorry,' Mrs Markham said. 'Can you remember, George?'

He shook his head.

'Have you always lived in this house?'

'Yes. All Sarah's life.'

'Except for the few months in Chicago.'

'Yes.'

'What did you do in Chicago?' I said.

'Do?'

'For a living?'

'Oh, I was at home,' Mrs Markham said.

'How about you, Mr Markham?'

'I worked in radio,' he said.

'Really?' I said. 'On air?'

'Yes. I was the studio announcer.'

'At a station in Chicago?' I said.

'Yes,' he said.

'Do you remember the station?'

'No, not really,' Mr Markham boomed. 'I worked at several.'

'You don't remember where you worked?'

He smiled sadly and shook his head.

'I, we, neither of us has much of a memory for things. I'm sure we must seem stupid to you.'

They didn't seem stupid. They seemed dishonest. But I knew if I stuck at it, all I would get was endless reaffirmation of their dishonesty. I smiled at them both.

'And since Chicago?' I said. 'What have you been working at since Chicago?'

'Oh, I work from home.'

'Really,' I said. 'What kind of work?'

'I manage our portfolio,' he said. 'The internet makes it so much easier to do.'

'You live on your investments?'

'Yes. I made some wise' – he chuckled – 'perhaps lucky, investments when we were in Chicago and...' He shrugged modestly.

'And you've lived off it ever since?'

'George is very good at investing,' Mrs Markham said.

'I'll bet he is,' I said.

We stood. We walked to the door. We shook hands. They stood in the doorway as I walked down the front walk toward my car.

They looked entirely forlorn.

George is very good at investing, I thought, *my ass!*

26

8

Dr Copeland had abandoned me to a female shrink in Cambridge, and now, looking for a parking space on Linnaean Street, I was on my way to my first appointment. I was carefully dressed for the event in a Donna Karan pinstriped suit. Nothing flashy. We were going to be two professionals, talking.

Like everywhere else in Cambridge, it is hard to park on Linnaean Street, and like every other appointment I ever had, I was late. I finally squeezed my car in near a hydrant and walked very fast. Her office was on the first floor of a big white Victorian with a porch. I had all the instructions. Enter without knocking, take a seat in the waiting room on the left.

There was a white-sound machine in the waiting room. And a stack of *New Yorker* magazines. The room had probably once been a parlor, and a big green-tiled fireplace took up much of one wall. There was a mirror above the fireplace, and I made sure my hair was neat and my lipgloss wasn't too glossy. Then I sat and picked up an issue of *The New Yorker* and opened it in my lap so I could avoid eye contact with any client that might go past me.

A door across the hall opened, and then the front door opened and closed, and then I heard a voice.

'Miss Randall?'

I stood up quickly.

'Yes,' I said.

'Hi,' the voice said, 'I'm Dr Silverman.'

I put my magazine down on the table. She gave me a little beckoning gesture and led me into her office, gestured me to a chair, closed the office door firmly, and went around her desk and sat. The first thing I noticed was how good-looking she was, and how subtly well dressed she was. How understated but careful her makeup was. She seemed like a woman. I felt like a girl.

'Tell me why you're here,' Dr Silverman said.

'My husband, my former husband, is remarrying.'

Dr Silverman nodded.

'Has it happened?'

'It's about to.'

'And you feel bad?'

'It is breaking my heart,' I said.

'Are you suicidal?' she said.

I paused and thought about it.

'No,' I said. 'I'm just very, very unhappy.'

'We should be able to improve that,' she said.

I nodded. I could feel the tears again. Isn't this wonderful – go to see a new shrink and start to cry thirty seconds after you meet her.

'What is your former husband's name?' Dr Silverman said.

'Richie.'

'Tell me about you and Richie,' she said.

I began. Halfway through, I started to cry. I tried to swallow it. I couldn't. Dr Silverman pushed a box of Kleenex across the desk to me. I used them and talked and cried and talked until Dr Silverman said gently, 'We've run out of time for today.'

I nodded and made a weak attempt at pulling myself together.

'Do you see any hope for me, doctor?'

'Let's not get ahead of ourselves,' Dr Silverman said.

The cliché annoyed me.

'No,' I said. 'We wouldn't want to do that.'

'Next week, then?' she said. 'Same time?'

'Would it be better if I came more than once a week?' I said.

'Would you like to?' Dr Silverman said.

'I am not going to continue to be the sniveling reject I feel like right now,' I said. 'I am going to beat this thing. I am going to get well.'

'Why don't you come in on Monday, then?' Dr Silverman said. 'And Thursday.'

'I will.'

She wrote out a little appointment card for me. I took it and put it in my purse with my gun.

'We've been divorced five years,' I said. 'We've both had other relationships. Why is this so hard?'

'We'll see if we can find out,' Dr Silverman said and stood and walked me to the door.

9

I was feeling a little less disintegrated as I went out to Taft to talk with Sarah. It wasn't that Dr Silverman had done anything much but listen and say noncommittal things. But I felt, somehow, a little safer.

Sarah was wearing multicolored tights today with a short tank top and a lot of bare belly. She was slim enough to get away with it. But even though it was flat, her belly looked soft, and so did her spandex-squeezed butt. We sat on a stone bench outside the main entrance to the library, so Sarah could smoke.

'So tell me your earliest memory.' I said.

Sarah shrugged.

'I don't know.'

'Sure you do,' I said. 'Everyone has an early memory.'

'But how do you know it's your earliest?'

I took in some of the fall air, trying not to get cigarette smoke in there with it.

'Good point,' I said. 'Let me rephrase. Tell me something you remember from when you were very young.'

'I don't know.'

'Do you remember anything before you moved to Andover?'

'No.'

'Do you remember ever living anywhere else but the house where your parents live now?'

'Adopted parents,' Sarah said.

'Well, if we're going to be exact,' I said, 'they would be your adopt*ive* parents, you would be their adopt*ed* child.'

'Whatever,' Sarah said.

'So what do you remember?' I was positively perky.

'Nothing much,' Sarah said.

My perkiness slipped a little.

'Oh, fuck you,' I said.

She actually rocked back a little on the bench.

'Excuse me?' she said.

'Fuck you,' I said. 'You hire me to do a tough job, and you won't help me do it.'

'I'm not getting paid.'

'No, you idiot,' I said. 'You're paying me to find out something that you're preventing me from finding out.'

'Huh?'

'You don't want to work or think. You want to sit there like a lump and wait for me to hand you the solution.'

'Lump?'

'Lump,' I said. 'If I'm going to help you, you have to pitch in.'

'You're supposed to be the fucking detective,' she said.

'Well, at least we speak the same language,' I said. 'The only place I have to start is you and your possibly adoptive parents. And they're much more helpful than you are.'

'What did they say?'

'Nothing,' I said.

'But you said... oh, I get it.'

'Dynamite,' I said. 'Tell me the name of one of your friends when you were little.'

'You don't have to get all pissed off about it.'

'No,' I said, 'I don't. I choose to. Tell me something or I quit.'

She started to speak and stopped and took a long, movieish drag on her cigarette.

'I used to hang around with Bobby O'Brien,' she said.

'Boy or girl?'

'Boy.'

'You know where he lives now?'

'No.'

'Did you go to school together?'

'Yes.'

'Did you remain friends?'

'Until high school,' she said.

30

'What happened?'

'He got a girlfriend.'

'And you couldn't remain friends?'

Sarah shrugged. She dropped her cigarette on the ground and rubbed it out with her foot. There was a sand bucket for cigarette butts next to her.

'But he graduated in your class?'

'I guess.'

She took out another cigarette and tried to light it in the faint breeze. It took four matches. My father, when he had smoked, used to be able to cup the match in his hand and light the cigarette on the first try. None of the few women I knew who smoked could get one going in any outdoor setting. I wondered why. I was pretty sure if I smoked cigarettes I'd learn how to get one lit even in the wind. I was pretty sure it didn't have to be a guy thing.

'Parents still live in your neighborhood?' I said.

'I don't know.'

'Anyone else you used to play with as a kid?'

'Judy Boudreau.'

'Do you know where she is now?'

'No.'

'Graduate from high school with you?'

'Yes.'

'Anyone else?'

We went through this exercise for about twenty minutes, and I ended with a list of maybe twelve names. All of them racked out of her as though they were sworn secrets.

'So,' Sarah said. 'You happy now?'

'It's a start,' I said.

'So why do you want those names?'

'Because I want to talk with them.'

'Why?'

'In hopes it will help me find out who your biological parents are,' I said.

'How would they know?'

'I don't know,' I said. 'Being a detective is mostly about not knowing, and asking and looking until you do know, at least something.'

'You got a gun?' Sarah said.

'Yes.'

'You got it with you?'

'Yes.'

'Can I see it?'

'No.'

'I bet you don't really have one,' Sarah said.

I nodded.

'Who was your pediatrician?' I said.

'See, you're changing the subject.'

'No, I'm getting back to it. Pediatrician?'

'Dr Marks,' she said.

'As in Karl?' I said.

'Who?'

'How do you spell it?'

'I don't know.'

'Was he in Andover?'

'Yes. I'll bet you don't have a gun.'

There was no real reason not to show it to her, except that she had no need to see it, and I'd had a bad week, and expected to have a bad month, and I didn't feel like showing it to her.

'Anything else you can remember that might be useful?'

'If you had it you'd show it,' Sarah said. 'You don't have one.'

I stood.

'Do you know what your father does for a living?'

'Stepfather.'

'How does he make money?' I said.

'He buys and sells stocks and stuff.'

'Where'd the original investment come from?'

'I dunno.'

'Of course you don't,' I said.

'Well, you don't have to give me attitude about it.'

'You're right,' I said. 'If you think of anything, call me.'

'Sure.'

'Have a nice day,' I said.

I walked down the center of the library quadrangle and across the street to the lot where I'd parked. When I drove out of the lot I could see her up there, where I'd left her. Sitting on the bench, hunched a little against the coolness. Smoking.

10

'You've heard me speak of Tony Gault?' I said to Dr Silverman.

'Yes.'

'He was in town again last week.'

Dr Silverman nodded.

'We weren't intimate.'

'Though you have been in the past?'

'Yes. Several times.'

Dr Silverman nodded.

'In the past, did you enjoy intimacy?'

'Yes.'

'But not this time.'

'This time I couldn't.'

'Why not?'

'I don't know.'

Dr Silverman smiled and waited.

'I don't,' I said.

'What has changed?'

'Changed? For God's sake, Doctor, you know what has changed. Richie got married.'

Dr Silverman nodded.

'And what does that have to do with you and Tony Gault?'

'Well, for God's sake, I can't...'

Dr Silverman was quiet, her big eyes resting on me without movement, her hands settled quietly in her lap. She had a wide mouth and her lips were full. She was wearing a dark suit today. She didn't wear a wedding ring. I wondered if she was married. I wondered if she had a boyfriend. I wondered if she colored her hair. She must. She was definitely old enough to be coloring her hair. Great body, though. She must work out a lot. She probably had a boyfriend. Probably some Harvard geek.

Dr Silverman smiled and tilted her head forward a little.

'You can't... ?' she said.

'Well, I mean I don't want to get involved with Tony Gault.'

'Had that been a problem previously?'

'Involvement?' I said.

'Has he previously wanted more than intimacy?'

'No.'

'Then?' Dr Silverman said. 'This time?'

'Well, Richie was married.'

'Did Tony know that?'

'No.'

Dr Silverman was quiet for a moment. So was I. Then she leaned toward me a little more and smiled widely. It was a genuine smile, full of warmth and interest.

'So,' Dr Silverman said. 'What's up with that?'

I was quiet for a while.

Then I said, 'But I knew that.'

Dr Silverman nodded.

'You'd think it would be the other way around,' I said.

Dr Silverman didn't say anything.

'You'd think once Richie was gone,' I said, 'that I'd be more willing.'

Dr Silverman was quiet.

'But I'm not,' I said.

Dr Silverman might have nodded. It was so slight a nod that I wasn't sure.

'Not just Tony,' I said. 'I don't feel like I want to be intimate with anybody.'

Another nod... maybe.

'I have been...' I said. 'I've been intimate with a number of men since the divorce.'

Nod?

'Including Richie,' I said.

Dr Silverman seemed comfortable, tipped back in her chair slightly. Her hands were motionless in her lap. She seemed interested, in a pleasant, noncommittal kind of way. She was agreeable, but she was silent. I wanted her to talk. I wanted her to explain me. I didn't know what to say. Dr Silverman didn't seem to mind. She was comfortable with the silence.

'Richie was protection,' I said.

She leaned forward a little.

'Tell me about that,' she said.

'As long as he was… as long as I could love him, even though we were divorced, I was safe. I could go out with other men, have sex, whatever. And I would not have to worry about anything beyond that.'

'What might be beyond that?' Dr Silverman said.

I was quiet. Then I said, 'Marriage, I guess.'

11

Of the twelve names I had wrenched from Sarah, four were still around. One of them was Bobby O'Brien, the name she'd mentioned first. I talked with him at the pub in the student union at Templeton College.

'You sure don't look like a detective,' Bobby said.

'I'm in disguise,' I said.

'It's working good,' Bobby said.

He was a chunky kid with a rust-colored crew cut and a flat nose.

'You look like a hockey player,' I said.

'Yep.'

'How are you in the corners?' I said.

Bobby grinned. 'Terrifying,' he said.

'You went to school with Sarah Markham,' I said.

'Sarah? Sure. First grade on.'

'Do you see much of her anymore?'

He shook his head.

'Tell me about her.'

'Whaddya want to know?' Bobby said.

'Anything you can tell me. What she was like, what her family is like, anything that strikes you.'

'And why do you want to know?'

I thought about it. No one had sworn me to secrecy, and the more the question was out there, the more chance that someone might think of something.

'We're trying to establish if she's adopted.'

'Adopted?'

'Yes.'

'She doesn't know?'

I shook my head.

'Her mother and father don't know?'

'They say she's not adopted. We're just trying to establish it for sure.'

'Man,' Bobby said. 'That's weird.'

'Because?' I said.

'I mean, you live your whole life with your mother and father, and then you all of a sudden think maybe they're not? What the hell is that about?'

'We're looking into that,' I said. 'What was she like in school?'

'Fine. She was pretty smart, and kind of popular and, you know, was part of the right group until maybe seventh grade.'

'And then?'

'She started hanging with the frazz-outs.'

'Frazz-outs?'

'Losers, dopeheads, dropouts, the bad crowd.'

'Oh,' I said, 'those frazz-outs. She do drugs?'

Bobby looked down at his thick, freckled hands resting in front of him on the chipped Formica tabletop.

'I don't like talking about her,' he said.

'Why not?'

'It feels like I'm ratting her out.'

'I work for her,' I said. 'She's paying me to ask these kinds of questions.'

He nodded.

'Yeah, she did a lot of drugs. Still does, I'm pretty sure.'

'Was she... sexually promiscuous?'

'She was pretty slutty in high school,' he said.

'Did you ever go out with her?'

'A little,' he said.

'Did you ever sleep with her?'

'Hey.'

'I told you,' I said, 'I'm a detective.'

He nodded again.

'Yeah. I slept with her. Once. Then it was over. She wouldn't go out with me again.'

'Did she not want you to sleep with her?'

'That's the funny part,' Bobby said. 'She was hot. It was her idea, but after we did it, she didn't want to see me anymore.'

'What did she say?'

'That's how weird it was. She didn't say anything. She just got up, put herself back together, you know, got out of the car, and walked away.'

'She told me she stopped seeing you because you got a girlfriend.'

'I got a girlfriend, but that was a long time after I had anything to do with Sarah.'

'Do you know if she was this way with anyone else?'

'Lotta guys,' Bobby said. 'It was like she wanted you to do it to her, and when you did it, she didn't like you anymore.'

'To her,' I said.

'Whaddya mean?'

'It sounds as if she didn't enjoy it,' I said.

'No. Not when it was happening, just before.'

'Is there someone I could talk with who knows her now?'

'Her college roommate. They go to Taft together.'

'And her name is?'

'Polly Murphy,' he said. 'What's all this got to do with whether her parents adopted her or not?'

'I have no idea,' I said.

12

I talked with Bobby O'Brien for another half hour but didn't learn anything more. Over the next few days, I talked with the other classmates she had mentioned, and a few she hadn't. Several of them agreed with Bobby, that she had changed when she was thirteen. No one had any theories why. No one could give me any information about her parentage. No one had ever heard her question it.

I met Sarah for coffee at Taft. Sarah took hers black.

'What happened to you,' I said, 'when you were thirteen?'

'Huh?'

'When you were thirteen, in the seventh grade, something happened.'

'What?'

'I was hoping you'd know,' I said.

Sarah lit a cigarette and took in a lot of smoke and let it out, slowly looking at it as it floated between us.

'I don't know what you're talking about,' she said. 'You find anything out yet about my parents?'

'Not much,' I said.

'Well, whyn't you do that and stop nosing around about me in the seventh grade?'

'Something happen that made you start to wonder about your parents?'

'In the seventh grade?'

'Yes.'

'No,' she said. 'I always knew they weren't my parents.'

I nodded. Sarah drank some black coffee. I sipped some of mine. Even with milk and two sugars, it was harsh and unpleasant. Drunk black, it must have been appalling.

'You just knew?' I said.

'Yes. I told you that. I always knew. You think I wouldn't know. You know things like that.'

I looked at my coffee. I didn't drink it.

'Sarah?' I said.

'Sarah what?' she said, and dropped her cigarette butt forcefully into her coffee. 'Why don't you stop bugging me like I did something bad? I didn't do anything wrong. Whyn't you find out what you're supposed to find out?'

'We're not supposed to be adversaries,' I said.

'Well, then, stop snooping on me,' Sarah said.

She lit another cigarette.

'Stop snooping on me,' she said.

I nodded. Tears began to well up in Sarah's eyes. She started to cry in little soft gasps. I put a hand out and patted her arm. She yanked the arm away and hugged herself. I tried to feel bad for her, and couldn't. There was nothing in our conversation that constituted a reasonable basis for crying. She was always on the verge of hysteria.

'I won't snoop on you,' I said.

It didn't slow her much. She cried and smoked and didn't say anything. I sat and waited and didn't say anything, either.

Everything about Sarah and her parents seemed fraudulent. And more than that, insubstantial, like something that had been built on the cheap, with shoddy materials and no craft, to conceal something unhealthy and mean.

It's not like my life is going really swell, either, honey.

I shook my head. *Stop it.* There was nothing in that direction that would do anyone any good. After a while she stopped crying, and even let me pat her forearm a couple times. She lit another cigarette, and then stood up quite suddenly.

'I have to go now,' she said, and turned and walked away.

Which is probably what I should have done.

13

In the bright morning, with the sun streaming through my skylight, as I drank coffee, with Rosie watching closely, I sat at my kitchen table and started on the phone. By the time I got through, it was late afternoon. I had drunk too much coffee. The sun had moved to the west. And I had talked with the American Federation of Television and Radio Artists' New York office, its LA office, the media columnists in both Chicago papers, a guy at WGN who had a late-night jazz show and was said by one of the media columnists to know everyone who'd worked in radio in Chicago since Marconi, and a woman I'd known in art school a long time ago, who had since married and moved to Chicago. As far as anyone knew, no one named George Markham had ever worked in radio in Chicago.

Late in the afternoon, eastern daylight saving time, when it was already getting dark in Boston, however, a particularly diligent clerk in the Los Angeles AFTRA office found a George Markham who had worked at a radio station in the Quad Cities in 1982. I called the radio station and got a recorded message. If I wanted to connect with the Dave Dixon show and be part of the Talk of Quad Cities, I could call an 800 number. I was pretty sure Dave wouldn't be helpful.

Rosie was sitting, staring at the kitchen counter. I got up and fed her and poured myself some wine and went back to the table and looked out the window. Four stories down, some headlights moved slowly toward Fort Point Channel. People going home to supper. There was some neon in a sandwich shop window down the block. I got up and walked down the length of my loft and looked for a time at the painting I was working on, of the South Station facade. I had no idea if it was good or not. Once I started a painting, I lost all ability to judge it. Maybe if I did enough paintings and sold them, I'd be able to trust my instincts and be less uncertain. Now all I could do was plow along.

Except for the noise Rosie made eating her supper, the loft was silent. I drank the rest of my wine and walked back to the kitchen area and filled the glass again. I thought about Dr Silverman. There was something about her, some sort of unspoken energy. I felt like I might like her. If she had a boyfriend, maybe he wasn't a Harvard geek.

I drank some wine. Rosie finished her supper and came

across the loft and jumped on the bed. I walked over and patted her. She rolled over on her back so I could rub her stomach.

'I too can have a relationship,' I said.

I sat for a while, patting her and drinking my wine. Then I got up again and walked to the window and looked out some more, at nothing much.

Obviously, there was something wrong in the Markham household if George had lied about where he worked. Of course it could be another George Markham... in the same business... in the same state... during the time when Sarah was born.

I went to the counter and poured some more wine.

It was a given that I loved Richie. I had loved him since I met him, and I loved him now. *So tell me, Doctor, why did I divorce him? Maybe I should be first asking why I married him? Okay, doctor. I married him because I loved him... or because he loved me... or because he wanted to marry me so much... or if I hadn't married him, I'd have lost him. So I had to marry him, even though I didn't want to get married... and I was right: I shouldn't be married. Why not? What was her first name? Susan. You tell me, Dr Susan. Isn't that what you're supposed to do? No, I know, you're supposed to help me answer that... God, you are in my head already. Asking why I married him brings me right around to asking why I divorced him.*

I could see my reflection in the dark window. I made a toasting gesture at me.

Maybe you're pretty smart, Dr Susan... Maybe I'm pretty smart, too... Maybe we'll figure this out... Maybe I'll be intimate *with somebody... Maybe Richie's new marriage won't* work... Maybe it won't matter, because I can never be with somebody... Maybe I'm drunk.

I looked at myself in the glass for a little bit longer, and then I went to the sink and threw my wine away and walked to the bed and lay down, still dressed, and went to sleep with Rosie.

14

I called Richie on his cell phone.

'I have to go out of town for a few days,' I said. 'Could you take Rosie?'

'Sure, bring her over,' Richie said. 'It's time for my custody days, anyway.'

I didn't want to bring her over. I didn't want to encounter my replacement.

'You're in Marblehead now?'

'Yep. You need the address?'

I knew the address.

'Yes,' I said. 'You'd better give it to me.'

He did.

'Are you coming out now?'

'Yes. Be there in an hour.'

'Okay,' Richie said. 'I'll wait for you.'

I knew why he was waiting, so I wouldn't have to leave Rosie with his new wife, whom I'd never even met. Maybe she wouldn't be there.

It took less than an hour, through the Ted Williams Tunnel and up Route 1A. I got there early. Richie had a big house up in the rocks with a view of the ocean. I had never been there. Whenever Rosie visited, Richie had always picked her up on his way home. I drove past the house and U-turned and parked where Rosie and I could look at the ocean near Preston Beach. I had left home at 9:15. It was now only ten minutes to ten. I would have died before I would have arrived in less than an hour. There were twenty-five minutes to kill. The day was brisk and sunny with some wind. The water looked bright and cold. Rosie had gotten down on the floor and curled up tightly, near the heater vent, and gone to sleep. A couple gulls lingered in the air above the interface of beach and ocean. There were always gulls.

At 10:13, I put the car in gear and backed out and drove to Richie's house. At 10:17, I was parked at the top of his steep driveway. I felt as if my soul had fallen into something bottomless. Rosie knew where she was and pranced as we went to the front door, with her tail wagging very fast. When Richie opened the door, she was ecstatic and did several bull terrier spins. Behind Richie was a slender blonde woman. The blonde crouched down, and Rosie rushed over and squeaked a little. The blonde put her face down, and Rosie lapped it. Squeaks and a lap – Sweet Jesus!

'Sunny, this is my wife, Kathryn,' Richie said. 'Kathryn, Sunny Randall.'

Kathryn stood. *Christ,* I thought, *she looks like me.* We shook hands.

'It's lovely to finally meet you,' Kathryn said.

'And it's lovely to meet you,' I said.

I hated her with every strand of DNA in my being. And, of course, she knew it.

'Would you care for a house tour?' Kathryn said. 'We've just done some rehab upstairs.'

'I'd love to,' I said. 'But I have to catch a plane to Chicago.'

'Oh, well, next time.'

'Sure,' I said.

'We'll take good care of Rosie,' Kathryn said. 'She's a wonderful dog.'

'Yes,' I said. 'Isn't she?'

Richie's face had no expression. Rosie was on the couch now, lying on her back, with her short legs in the air. I went over and sat for a moment and rubbed her stomach and bent over and gave her a kiss.

'You be a good girl,' I said. 'I'll be back soon.'

Rosie wagged her tail. I stood.

'I should be back by Friday,' I said. 'I'll call.'

'Rosie is always welcome,' Kathryn said.

'Thanks, Kathryn,' I said. 'It's been great meeting you.'

We shook hands again. I gave Richie a kiss on the cheek and left.

Kathryn seemed very nice. Richie loved her. And Rosie liked her. *How bad could she be?*

I drove to the airport, parked in the garage, and got a 1:30 flight to Chicago. I passed the two-hour flight thinking about ways to kill Kathryn without getting caught.

15

There were planes from Chicago to the Quad Cities, but I was certain they would be small and scary, and I chose to rent a car. The drive from O'Hare Airport is almost due west across the Illinois prairie, where the flat farmland is made various only now and then by the rise of a silo or the bigger rise of a grain elevator. I got there about seven o'clock in the evening, and checked into a motel in Moline, near the Quad Cities airport. Moline was on the east bank of the Mississippi River, along with Rock Island. Bettendorf and Davenport were in Iowa, west of the river.

Talk Radio WMOL was located in a low cinder-block building on John Deere Road, and in the morning, I went over there. I spent some time in the reception area, while the receptionist tried to figure out whom I should talk to. And I waited some more while the person I should talk to decided if he wanted to talk with me. While I waited, I had to listen to the current program broadcasting on WMOL. It was a call-in show. The host was discussing abortion with callers. The program didn't seem very controversial to me. The host was opposed to abortion and so were all the callers. I looked at the photos of the on-air talent on the wall near the reception desk. There was a woman and three men. The woman and two of the men looked young. WMOL was probably a stepping stone. The third man looked old. For him, WMOL was probably a stepping stone in the other direction.

Finally, a small, neat young man in a white shirt and a red tie came into the reception area and looked at me.

'Miss Randall?'

'Yes.'

'Hi, I'm Jeff. I'm the station manager,' he said, and gestured toward the door behind him. 'Come on in.'

Jeff's office was small, and there were more pictures on the wall. The on-air personalities were there, and a lot of other pictures that were meaningless to me except for a picture of Adlai Stevenson shaking hands with someone in front of the WMOL building, and a youthful-looking publicity still of Lolly Drake in front of a WMOL microphone.

'She worked here?' I said.

'Fresh out of law school,' Jeff said. 'Half-hour call-in at noon. She answered legal questions.'

'I'll be damned,' I said.

'Everybody's got to start someplace,' Jeff said.

'You hope,' I said.

'I do indeed. How can I help you?'

'I'm looking for a man who appears to have worked here in the early 1980s,' I said. 'Man named George Markham.'

'Hell,' Jeff said. 'In the early eighties, I was in grammar school.'

I nodded.

'Do you have personnel records?'

'Probably, somewhere,' Jeff said. 'But I got something better.'

He leaned over his desk and pressed an intercom button and said, 'Millie, could you come in here?'

Then he leaned back and grinned at me.

'I got Millie,' he said. 'Millie was here when Adlai Stevenson cut the ribbon.'

Millie, when she came in, was tall and angular and sort of mean-looking, with a lot of small wrinkles on her hard face. Her hair was gray and curly and cut short. Her cheeks had the sunken look of a longtime smoker.

'Whaddya need, Jeffy?' she said, and sat down next to me.

Jeff glanced down at my card on his desk to refresh his memory.

'Sunny Randall, Millie McNeeley.'

Millie reached across and gave me a hard handshake.

'Nice meetin' ya,' she said. Her voice was raspy.

'Miss Randall is a detective from Boston.'

'No shit?' Millie said. 'A girl detective?'

'Me and Nancy Drew,' I said. 'Do you remember George Markham?'

'George? Sure. He was an announcer here, you know, the booth guy.' She dropped her raspy voice and cupped a hand behind her ear. *'This is WMOL, Quad City Sound.'*

'We say "Quad City Talk" now,' Jeff said.

I took a picture of George Markham out of my purse and held it up.

'Is this him?' I said.

Millie had reading glasses on a string around her neck. She put them on and took the picture and looked at it, holding it away from her as far as she could.

'Sure,' she said. 'That's George. Wow, he sure didn't get better-looking as he got older, did he?'

'Was he good-looking when you knew him?'

'Oh, you bet,' Millie said, 'Twenty years ago. I had a little yen for him myself.'

'Did anything work out?' I said.

Millie grinned at me.

'None of your damn business,' she said.

'Of course it's not,' I said. 'Was he married then?'

'His wife was,' Millie said.

'But he fooled around?'

'I'm not one to tell tales out of school,' Millie said.

'And he worked here in 1981?'

'Lemme see, it was around the same time as Lolly. She came in 1980. He was here in '79 and left in… '84.'

'Did he have a child?' I said.

'Not that I know about.'

'Was his wife pregnant?'

'I only saw her a couple of times when she'd come to the station. A real pickle-puss.'

'She look pregnant?'

'No.'

'So what was he like?'

Millie took a pack of Chesterfield cigarettes, the long, unfiltered ones, shook one loose, took it from the package with her mouth, tossed the pack on the desk, and lit the cigarette with a Zippo lighter. She took a deep inhale, let the smoke out in little smoke rings, took the cigarette out of her mouth, and held it between the first two fingers of her right hand.

'He was a slick one,' Millie said.

She'd been holding cigarettes for a long time. The fingers holding this one were nicotine-stained.

'Like how?' I said.

'Well, he let you know that he was just passing through here. Let you know he'd worked a lot of big markets, and knew a lot of big-time people.'

'But he was working here,' I said.

'Hey,' Jeff said.

I smiled.

'Sorry,' I said. 'But...' I shrugged.

'Yeah, yeah,' Jeff said. 'I know.'

'Did he say where he'd worked before?' I said.

'Nope. He was a little older than most of the girls who worked here, except for me, and he spent a lot of time snowing them about how he'd worked with William B. Williams in New York, or Milt Rosenberg in Chicago.'

'You believe him?'

She snorted and took a drag on her Chesterfield.

'Hell, no,' she said. 'He just wanted to get their pants off.'

'Did he succeed?'

Millie shrugged.

'Got no way to know,' she said.

'Well,' I said, 'it certainly sounds like he fooled around on his wife.'

'I'm not saying he did, or didn't.'

'And,' I said, 'as far as you know, there were no children?'

'Far as I know. 'Course, I never went to his house or anything.'

'Did anyone? Was he close to anyone that might still be around?'

'None that I know of.'

'This is a transient business,' Jeff said.

''Cept for old Millie,' Millie said. 'Been here since 1950. Started as a typist right out of high school. Station played Patti Page music.'

'The singing rage,' I said.

'You're older than you look,' Millie said.

'Not really. My friend Spike has all her old records.'

'God knows why,' Millie said.

'God knows,' I said. 'Did you like George Markham?'

Millie thought about that for a minute, while smoking her Chesterfield.

'No,' she said. 'I didn't. He was kind of cute and sexy, but you got past that. He was the kind of guy willing to spend his life saying, "This is WMOL Quad City Sound."'

'"Talk,"' Jeff said.

'He'd be a nice night?' I said. 'A terrible week?'

Millie smiled a big smile at me.

'You know the type,' she said.

'I do,' I said. 'Too well.'

16

'I'm not her roommate anymore,' Polly Murphy said.

We were talking softly at a table in the main library reading room at Taft.

'Why?' I said.

'Well… I guess I thought I would study better.'

'So you moved in with someone else?'

'Yes. Maxine Goetz.'

Polly was cute. Her weight would probably become an issue in a few years. Right now it wasn't. She had thick, dark hair, which she wore like Catherine Zeta-Jones, and probably shouldn't have. And her teeth were very white.

I smiled at her.

'Maxine is a studier,' I said.

'Yes. She's been dean's list every semester.'

'You?'

She looked down modestly. 'Most.'

'Good for you,' I said.

'My parents are paying good money to send me here,' Polly said. 'I think they deserve my best effort.'

Wow!

I looked at her for a minute to see if she was teasing me. She seemed sincere.

'How about Sarah?'

'She was more of a party girl,' Polly said.

'When I was in college that meant basically beer and boys,' I said.

'Well, Sarah liked that, certainly.'

'She bring it back to the room too much?'

Polly shrugged.

'You and she were childhood friends?' I said.

She nodded.

'All through high school?'

Polly nodded again.

'Even after she changed?'

'You know about her?' Polly said.

'Just what I hear,' I said. 'I heard she was kind of a smart, sweet girl until junior high.'

'I know what people said about her,' Polly said. 'But she was my friend.'

I nodded.

'We decided to come to Taft to stay with each other.'

I nodded again. 'But...' I said.

'It was... very difficult... living with her,' Polly said.

'Beer and boys?'

'Some of that...'

'And?'

Polly leaned across the table, closer to me.

'Sarah took a lot of drugs.'

'More than grass?' I said.

'Oh, yes. Hard drugs.'

'Like what?'

'I don't know. I don't use drugs.'

'Good for you,' I said.

'I graduate this June, and next year, I want to be in a really good MBA program. I don't want to do anything to spoil my chances.'

'So her drug use was disruptive?'

'Yes. She'd come in at night, late sometimes, and act crazy.'

'Like?'

'Like she'd be crying and seeing things and…' Polly shook her head. 'Did you ever go to college?'

'I did,' I said.

'What did you major in?'

'Art.'

'Really?'

I could tell that Polly found that puzzling.

'How did you do?'

'I was a good artist and quite a bad student,' I said.

'Really?' Polly said.

She frowned. I could see that she was puzzled again.

'Who does Sarah room with now?' I said.

'I don't know. Different people, I think. You know? Boys, mostly.'

'She got a boyfriend?' I said.

'No, not really. I guess she plays the field.'

'Where does she get her drugs?'

'I don't know. I mean it's a college, you know? I mean anybody can get drugs at a college.'

'Any one person?'

Polly shrugged and shook her head.

'Sarah ever talk about her parents?' I said.

'Not really. I don't think she liked her mom much.'

'How about her father?'

'I think she liked him.'

'She say why she didn't like her mother?'

Polly shrugged again. 'I think she thought her mom didn't like her.'

She shook her head. Incomprehensible.

'You know her mother?' I said.

'Oh, yes.'

'You think she liked Sarah?'

'Well, of course,' Polly said. 'She was Sarah's mom.'

'Why do you suppose Sarah thought that?' I said.

'I don't know, Ms Randall. I really don't. I mean, walking around saying your mom doesn't like you. I think it's probably the drugs.'

'She's been doing drugs for a while, then?' I said.

'Yes, since junior high, probably. But then it was different. I didn't live with her. I didn't have to be there when she got crazy, or worry about all her druggie friends stealing my stuff.'

'She ever steal from you?'

Polly sighed. 'There were things that disappeared,' she said.

'Did you ever bring it up to her?'

'Yes.'

'What happened?'

'She told me if I didn't trust her, she didn't want me there, and I should get out.'

'And that's when you moved?' I said.

'Maxine's roommate moved in with her boyfriend, and so I went over there with Maxine. I felt bad leaving her. But she was so... sometimes she would have sex in the other bed... in the same room.'

'Ick,' I said.

'It's not goodie-goodie to not like that,' Polly said.

'No,' I said. 'It's human.'

17

'So when she reached seventh grade... which would be, what, twelve, thirteen... Everything went to hell.'

Dr Silverman nodded.

'And I can't find out if something happened.'

'You think something happened?'

'Everyone says she changed.'

'Perhaps puberty happened,' Dr Silverman said.

'I thought of that,' I said. 'But I went through puberty without becoming a drugged-out, promiscuous whack job. Didn't you?'

'Maybe she had more compelling reasons to become a whack job,' Dr Silverman said. 'Or more thoroughly a whack job.'

'So she might have had problems which didn't become evident until her chemistry changed?'

'Maybe,' Dr Silverman said.

'So, if puberty is a process of sexual maturation,' I said, 'are the problems associated with it sexual?'

'Often,' Dr Silverman said.

'Boy,' I said. 'It is hard to get a straight answer from you.'

'Getting answers from me is not our goal here,' Dr Silverman said.

'Oh, shit,' I said.

Dr Silverman raised her eyebrows and tilted her head a little.

'I'm sorry,' I said. 'I mean, I know that it's about me, not about you. You're just so goddamned shrinky.'

'I am, after all, a shrink.'

'I know, I know. There's just this know-it-all, goddamned, I'm-the-grownup-you're-the-child quality to it all.'

Dr Silverman leaned back in her chair. She was wearing a dark pinstripe suit today. Her nails gleamed with clear polish. She wore makeup. Which was good. I was uneasy about women who didn't wear makeup. But it was very understated makeup. Nothing flamboyant – don't want to jar the patient. With her hands clasped in her lap, she rubbed the tips of her thumbs together gently. I had already learned that that meant she had encountered something interesting.

'What?' I said.

'Do you really think I treat you like a child?' she said.

'Oh, hell, I don't know. I was just mad.'

'At what?'

I stared at her. She seemed almost eager as she leaned

forward in her chair, though I was pretty certain she wasn't. Without any real sign that I could pick up, she seemed to be cheering me on. She was like a herd dog: a lean here, an eyebrow there. Rub the thumbs. And all of a sudden, there it was. I was where I'm sure she wanted me to be.

'It's so corny I'm embarrassed,' I said.

Eyebrow. Head tilt.

'I'm mad at my mother,' I said.

Dr Silverman smiled. For her, that was like jumping in the air and clicking her heels.

'Let's talk about that a little,' she said.

'Does this mean you're not going to solve the Sarah Markham case for me?' I said.

She smiled. 'I'm afraid it does,' she said.

18

I had coffee and a cinnamon bun with George Markham in a Starbucks on Main Street in Andover.

'Have you been able to persuade my daughter to stop this madness?' George said.

'I've not tried,' I said.

'Well, you should,' George said. 'You're too good-looking to waste your time chasing phantoms.'

How charming.

'Tell me about your radio career,' I said.

He smiled modestly and shrugged.

'It was nothing much,' he said. 'I just got some lucky breaks along the way.'

'Tell me about it. I'm fascinated with radio,' I said.

'I was on Armed Forces Radio in 'Nam,' he said, 'and managed, when I got out, to segue right into a job in New York. WNEW. I worked with William B. Williams there, if you know who he is.'

'A legend,' I said.

'In Chicago, I got to work with Milt Rosenberg at WGN.'

'Wow,' I said. 'Mostly announcing?'

He nodded.

'And a lot of producing,' he said. 'I did some on-air fill-in for the hosts when they were on vacation or out with a cold or something. Later I went on to do network. Not as glamorous maybe as it once was in, you know, the heyday. But it paid good, and there was much less local programming politics, you know?'

'Oh,' I said, 'I can imagine. Do you miss radio?'

'No,' he said, 'not really. It was fun. But I'm happy now, managing my affairs, spending time with my wife. That was then. This is now.'

'I was in Quad Cities last week,' I said.

George looked at me blankly.

'They remember you fondly out there,' I said.

'Quad Cities?'

'Yep. Talked with Millie at WMOL. Quad City Sound.'

'Millie?'

'Yep. Said you were very handy with the women.'

'I've never been to Quad Cities in my life.'

'You were there in the early eighties. Same time Lolly Drake was starting out.'

'Lolly Drake?' he said. 'The syndicated talk-show broad?'

He was still sort of round-shouldered. But away from his wife, the furtive-nerd persona faded fast.

'Yes,' I said. 'They still talk about her out there.'

'I don't know anything about it or her or out there,' George said. 'I simply do not know what you are talking about.'

I took his picture out of my purse and held it up.

'Is this you?' I said.

'Yeah,' he said. 'Sure.'

'That's what Millie said.' I smiled at him. 'She said you hadn't gotten better looking in twenty years.'

'The hell with her,' George said, looking at the picture.

Then he looked at me.

'The hell with you too,' he said, and stood and walked out of Starbucks.

I thought when I had him cornered, that he was supposed to crack under my relentless pressure and confess. Instead he told me to go to hell, and stuck me with the check.

Maybe I should try rubbing my thumbs together.

19

In the fall, on clear days, the morning sun shined straight through my skylight until eleven. I usually painted then, to take advantage of it. While I did this, Rosie normally lay on the bed among the decorative pillows, on her back, with her head turned so that when she felt like it, she could open one black, beady eye and check on me. She was doing it this morning while I was layering gray shadows among the columns on the upper stories of my South Station front.

My doorbell rang. Rosie jumped from the bed and charged to the door and stood, barking. As often as I'd told her, she never got that the person ringing the doorbell was several flights down and outside the building. It was one of her few confusions. I walked over and pushed the intercom button.

'Hi,' I said.

'Sunny?'

'Yes.'

'It's Sarah. I need to come in.'

'Fourth floor,' I said. 'Elevator's right in front of you. Wait for me to buzz.'

I went to my door and watched through the peephole until I saw her get off the elevator. She was alone. I opened my door and she came in. Rosie stopped barking and was thrilled to see her the minute the door was opened. She did a couple happy spins. Sarah pushed past Rosie without paying any attention to her. Rosie looked slightly put out and went and sat by the kitchen counter in case anyone wanted to give her a cracker. Sarah's left eye was swollen nearly shut, and she had a darkening bruise on her left jawline.

'Wow,' I said.

'They beat me up,' she said. 'They came to my room and beat up my boyfriend and me.'

'Where's your boyfriend?'

'He ran off.'

'And who are they?'

'I don't know.'

'Did you tell the police?'

'No. I came right over here. I'm scared. I thought they were going to kill me or something.'

I closed my front door, and, mostly for effect, pushed the bar on the slide bolt into place. Then I went to my bedside table and got my gun, and brought it back and laid it near me on the countertop. That was for effect, too, mostly.

'Would you like some coffee?' I said.

'No… yes… yes, I would.'

She took out a cigarette and lit it. She didn't ask if I minded. It didn't seem the right time to say 'Thanks for not smoking.'

'Did anyone follow you here?' I said.

'Follow?'

'Yes. Might your assailants know you're here?'

'Here? My God. I don't know. Can they get in?'

'No,' I said.

She went to the window and peeked out at the street.

'I don't see anybody,' she said.

'You take cream and sugar?' I said.

She continued to look down at the street, standing to the side so that she wouldn't be seen.

'Just sugar.'

I brought the coffee over and put it on the breakfast table.

'The building is quite secure,' I said. 'And my loft is quite secure. And we have a phone to call the cops. And I'm quite a good shot.'

'I don't see anybody,' she said.

'Good,' I said. 'Have some coffee. Tell me about it.'

Sarah left the window and sat across from me. Rosie came over and sat at my feet in case we were planning to eat

56

something. Sarah looked around the loft.

'You have a nice place,' she said.

'So what happened?'

'Well…' She drank some coffee and lit another cigarette. 'My boyfriend and I were partying in my room.'

'At the dorm?' I said.

'Yeah, sure, at the dorm.'

Partying could mean Hawaiian Punch, or beer or dope or sex or all of the above, though I was skeptical it meant Hawaiian Punch. On the other hand, the details of that could wait.

'And?' I said.

'And these two guys came in without knocking or anything and told my boyfriend to beat it, and he said, like, "Why?" And one of the guys punched him out.'

'Can you describe these guys?'

'Sort of,' she said. 'One of them was straight-looking, like a lawyer or an accountant, you know? Slim. Thick glasses. Dark suit. Tie. The other guy was bigger. He had on a leather jacket.'

'Was it the bigger man who punched out your boyfriend?' I said.

'Yes. He was so quick. Poor Woody.'

'Then what?'

'Then the guy in the leather jacket put Woody in my closet and told him to stay there, and shut the closet door. And the slim guy said to me I should stop investigating my parents. And I was so scared I couldn't talk and all I could do was shake my head, like, you know, *I don't understand*. But he musta thought I meant *no, I wouldn't*, and he, like, nodded his head to the guy in the leather jacket, and the guy hit me twice and knocked me down. And the slim guy said something like, "It can get a lot worse than this." And I said, "I'll do whatever you want." And he said, "I told you what I want. Do it." And the leather-jacket guy put his foot on my, ah, between my legs, and he gave like a little shove and winked at me. The fucking guy winked at me! And they left.'

'And Woody?' I said.

With the remainder of her cigarette dangling from the

corner of her mouth, away from the bruise, she poured herself some more black coffee and dumped in maybe six spoonfuls of sugar. Then she dragged on the cigarette and took it from her mouth and exhaled and drank some more coffee.

'As soon as they left,' she said, 'Woody came out of the closet and ran away.'

'Well,' I said. 'I guess it's important to know one's limitations.' She shrugged.

'Do you remember anything else about the two men?' I said.

'I think the tough guy had some kind of tattoos on his hand?'

'What kind?'

'I don't know,' Sarah said. 'Just some blue letters, like on his knuckles.'

'Would you recognize them if you saw them again?'

'I don't want to see them again.'

'We could show you a lot of pictures,' I said.

Sarah shook her head.

'I want out,' she said. 'I want you to stop.'

I looked at Sarah for a moment. Then I got up and walked the length of my loft to the bedroom end and looked out the window at the warehouse next door. Rosie followed me and sat down. Finally, I stopped looking at the warehouse and turned and walked back to Sarah. With what sounded like a small anthropomorphic sigh of annoyance, Rosie stood and trotted back down behind me.

'I can protect you,' I said to Sarah.

'You? You're a girl. What are you going to do if these guys show up?'

'I could shoot them,' I said.

'You wouldn't dare.'

'Of course I would.'

'You ever shoot anybody?'

'Yes.'

She looked at me. 'I don't believe you,' she said.

I shrugged.

'Did you really shoot somebody?'

I nodded.

'Do you think you'll all of a sudden stop wondering whose kid you are?' I said.

'I don't care. I'm scared.'

'Of course you are scared. But doesn't this make it even more necessary to find out what's going on? Doesn't this tell you that someone doesn't want you to find out anything?'

'Jesus,' Sarah said.

'And if you don't find out now what the truth is, it will destroy your life.'

'She wouldn't hire somebody to beat me up,' Sarah said.

'She?' I said.

'My mother.'

'Mrs Markham?' I said.

'Yes. She always used to yell at me when I was bad that she wasn't my mother.' Sarah's eyes began to tear. 'And then, you know, later, she would come and tell me never to tell anyone, because if I did, they'd send me to an orphanage.'

Sarah started to cry.

'What did your father say?'

She had some trouble talking between sobs, but she got it out.

'I never dared tell him.'

'Did she ever say it in front of him?'

'Once,' Sarah spoke haltingly, struggling for control, 'they had a big fight... and I heard them and I went... and sat on the floor outside... and listened... and she said, "It's not like she's my blood"... and my father shushed her... "She might hear you."'

She stopped trying to talk and put both hands over her face and bent forward and simply cried. I was quiet. Rosie looked a little uneasy. Finally, the crying slowed. I waited. Finally, it stopped.

'I think you should go wash your face with cold water,' I said. 'It'll make you feel better.'

She nodded and didn't move.

'Down past the bedroom area,' I said.

She nodded again.

'Go,' I said. 'Then we'll talk. You won't have to do anything you don't want to do.'

Sarah stood slowly and walked down the length of the loft as if she was drunk.

'There's makeup in there,' I said. 'Feel free.'

She went into my bathroom. While she was gone, I emptied the saucer she'd been using as an ashtray, and made some more coffee.

20

We were on our third pot of coffee. She'd drunk most of it. But I'd drunk enough to make my nerves jitter. Sarah was through crying for now. She was smoking.

'But why can't we just do what they want and they'll leave us alone?'

'And you'll never know what's being covered up,' I said.

'So,' she said, 'I won't know. You didn't see the look in that man's face when he put his heel into my crotch.'

'He meant that look,' I said. 'He wanted you to feel not only scared but small and powerless.'

'Well, I am. Why not just face it and get on with my life?'

I leaned back in my chair and waved the cigarette smoke away from my face. If we were going to do much of this, we'd have to have some arrangement.

'Because,' I said, 'and you'll have to excuse the psychological jargon, you are a fucking mess.'

'What's that supposed to mean?' Sarah said.

'It means that you use too many drugs, and drink too much booze, and smoke too many cigarettes, and screw too many men you don't like.'

'Yeah, well maybe you'd be a little messed up, too, if you grew up like me.'

'I am messed up,' I said. 'It takes one to know one. But I'm trying to fix what's wrong with me. You're just going to walk away.'

'What's wrong with you?'

'I'll let you know,' I said, 'when I know. Right now it's about you. You let them scare us away from this and you can kiss any chance for happiness goodbye.'

She laughed an awful little laugh.

'Happiness?' she said.

'You can stay here with me,' I said. 'No one knows you're here. I can protect you. If we need them, I have friends who can protect you. If you'll let me, I will do this for you.'

'Where am I going to sleep?' she said.

'Fold-out bed,' I said. 'In the couch.'

Sarah flapped her hand to indicate the openness of my space.

'We'd live together in the same room?' Sarah said.

'I know. It's lousy, but it needs to be done.'

'Is there another bathroom?'

'No,' I said. 'We'll share.'

'Share one bathroom?'

'I know it's icky, but people do it.'

'I got no clothes or anything.'

'Some of my stuff will fit you. The rest I can buy for you.'

'I don't have any money with me.'

'I'll put it on my bill,' I said.

'And you promise I'll be safe?'

'You'll be safe,' I said.

'Why are you pushing me so hard to do this?'

'I care about you?'

Sarah laughed that awful little laugh again.

'You must really need the money,' she said. 'To do this.'

'That's it,' I said. 'The money.'

21

I had Rosie on her leash. I had my shoulder bag with my cell phone in it, and my makeup, and my gun. I was wearing a black satin trench coat with a notched leather collar. I had on my black Oakley wraparounds. I was ready, and I was looking really good.

'You have any problem, what will you do?'

'I'll call nine-one-one,' she said, 'and the cell-phone number for your friend Spike.'

'Call Spike first,' I said. 'He'll arrive quicker.'

'Okay.'

'Where's the number?' I said.

'On the little chalkboard by the phone. You're sure he'll come?'

'I've talked to him,' I said. 'He'll come.'

'How will I know it's him?'

'Big, with a beard. Looks sort of like a bear.'

'A bear?'

'Yes. When he rings the intercom, he'll give you his name.'

'Okay.'

'You'll be fine,' I said.

She was drinking more coffee and smoking more cigarettes and looking very small, sitting alone at my breakfast table, looking cautiously out the window.

'You will,' I said. 'No one knows you're here. The building is secure. My door is secure. Lock the deadbolt when I leave.'

'Could the dog stay?' Sarah said.

'She'd rather go with me,' I said. 'She likes to ride in the car.'

'You don't trust me with her?'

Actually, I didn't. But I saw no reason to say so.

'I bring her with me because she likes to go.'

Sarah looked a little puzzled at that concept, but she didn't say anything.

'Okay. Obviously, don't go out. There's stuff for sandwiches and things in the refrigerator.'

Sarah nodded. Rosie was staring at the door as if hoping it would melt.

'I'm going out and work on your problem,' I said. 'You have my cell-phone number.'

Sarah nodded again. Rosie gave a sharp, nasty yap.

'Okay,' I said. 'We're going.'

Sarah said, 'I can call you.'

'Call me whenever you need to,' I said.

'Even if I don't really have anything to say?'

'Even,' I said.

22

Rosie waited in the car.

I went in and sat with the Markhams in the silent living room of their soundless house. There were no lights on. The Markhams sat on the couch. He at one end, she at the other. I sat in the flowered easy chair. Dust motes drifted in the sunlight that came in from the front windows.

'Two men beat up your daughter yesterday,' I said.

'My God,' Markham said. 'Is she all right?'

'She is,' I said.

'Where is she?' Markham said.

'She's safe,' I said. 'Can you think of any reason why that would happen?'

'No. My God!'

'She probably made it up,' Mrs Markham said.

'Why would she do that?' I said.

'She makes up all kinds of stuff,' Mrs Markham said.

Well, well. The gloves were off.

'She does?' I said.

'All this nonsense about who her parents are. The girl is a born liar.'

Mr Markham stared at his wife for a moment and frowned.

'Come on, Barb!' he said.

'She is, George, and you'd know it, too, if you didn't always coddle her.'

'She did have some bruises,' I said.

'Probably one of her drug-addict boyfriends,' Mrs Markham said.

'She wasn't,' Markham said, 'you know, I mean, there was nothing else happened to her?'

'No,' I said.

'Why did they do it?' Markham said.

'They told her to stop investigating her parentage.'

'She's crazy,' Mrs Markham said. 'She's a crazy liar.'

All three of us were quiet. The dust motes drifted. The silence pressed in.

'Sequence,' I said finally, 'doesn't necessarily prove cause. But the beating happened shortly after I talked to you about your days in Moline.'

Mrs Markham looked quickly at her husband.

'Moline?' she said.

Mr Markham looked straight at me.

'I told you before,' he said. 'I've never been to Moline.'

'What is this about Moline?' Mrs Markham said to me.

'You lived there twenty years ago. Your husband was an announcer at WMOL.'

'That's crazy,' Mrs Markham said. 'I don't even know where Moline is.'

'Are you suggesting that I had something to do with Sarah getting hurt?' Mr Markham said.

'Did you mention our conversation to anyone?'

'No. Of course not. It was too absurd.'

'But if it were that absurd, wouldn't you tell people about it? Your wife, for instance. Wouldn't you say, maybe, like, "Gee, Barb, that crazy broad that Sarah hired claims we lived in Moline, Illinois"?'

'I don't waste time on foolishness,' Mr Markham said, 'Neither does my wife.'

'Well,' I said. 'Somebody, for some reason, doesn't want this investigation to go further. Can you imagine who that would be?'

Mr Markham took in some air.

'Of course, Barbara and I would like it to stop. It is painful for us. But you can't believe we would harm our own daughter.'

'She made the whole thing up,' Mrs Markham said.

'You could settle it with a simple DNA comparison,' I said.

'We will not dignify her lies like that,' Mrs Markham said.

I looked at Mr Markham; he shook his head. I stood.

'Well,' I said. 'I have a dog waiting for me.'

Neither of them stood.

'For what it is worth,' I said, 'your daughter is not quitting, and neither am I. Sooner or later we will know the truth, whatever the truth turns out to be.'

'The truth is,' Mrs Markham said, 'that she's a self-indulgent, spoiled, drug-addicted liar.'

I smiled at her.

'No more Mrs Nice Guy?' I said.

Mrs Markham didn't answer. Mr Markham said nothing. I had nothing else to say.

So I left.

23

'I could never understand why he loved her,' I said. 'She was so dumb and bossy and… what… self-centered, I guess.'

Dr Silverman was wearing a gray suit this morning, with a black turtleneck sweater.

'Tell me a little more about her,' Dr Silverman said.

A regular damn chatterbox today.

'My father pretends she's smart. He always acts like she's a wonder if she, you know, cooks a lamb chop, or finds her keys, or buys some cheap piece of fabric for the couch. He always acts as if no one else could have done it.'

'It must be annoying.'

'It is,' I said. 'And she always sort of acts like she's won some sort of contest when he does it.'

'Maybe she has,' Dr Silverman said.

'With me?' I said.

'You think?' Dr Silverman said.

'Yes. With me and my sister. For Daddy.'

Dr Silverman nodded. She appeared to understand everything. Of course, that could be training rather than truth.

Still, there was a great deal of warmth in her. I could feel it. And distance, too. I couldn't quite understand how she was both at the same time. She waited.

'Elizabeth is older,' I said. 'She didn't like me. I'm sure she resented me for being born.'

'How do you get along now?'

'We don't. We are connected because we're, you know, sisters. But we still don't really like each other.'

'Why?' Dr Silverman said.

'Why?'

She nodded.

'She's so much like my mother, I suppose. And more than anything else, she thinks you are a failure if you are not with a man.'

'Is she with one now?'

'Too many,' I said. 'She's divorced. She's desperate. She'll sleep with the first guy who offers.'

'How about you?' Dr Silverman said.

'After my divorce? No. I handled that pretty well. I slept with men if I liked them, and not if I didn't.'

'Until recently,' Dr Silverman said.

'Yes.'

We were quiet.

'Now I don't sleep with anybody.'

Dr Silverman was quiet. I was quiet. It wasn't so hard being quiet as it had been.

'How did you compare?' Dr Silverman said.

'To my mother and sister?'

She nodded. I smiled.

'Favorably,' I said.

'Talk about that,' she said.

'I was always good at things. I was an athlete. I rowed in college, single sculls. My father taught me how to shoot. I liked to go to ball games with him. I liked to talk about his work. My father was a cop. A captain when he retired. He used to take me in to work sometimes. I was kind of funny. I had dates. I was popular in school. My grades were okay. Not like Elizabeth's.

She got all A's every year. It impressed the hell out of my mother, but I sort of knew, and I think my father did, that grades are mostly bullshit. I got B's and C's without trying very hard.'

'It sounds like you were close to your father.'

'Yes.'

Then Dr Silverman said, 'Did your father prefer you?'

'You mean over my sister?'

'Or your mother,' she said.

I was quiet again, thinking about the answer. It wasn't that I didn't know the answer. It was trying to say it without sounding like a jerk. Finally, I settled for sounding like a jerk.

'He liked me best,' I said.

Dr Silverman nodded. We were quiet again. I felt very heavy inside.

'Are we getting oedipal here?' I said.

'What do you understand by the term "oedipal"?'

'Kill my mother and marry my father... symbolically of course.'

'Do you think we're getting oedipal?' Dr Silverman said.

'Hey,' I said. 'You're the oedipal expert.'

Dr Silverman smiled.

'He liked you best,' she said.

'Yes.'

'That could be quite burdensome for a young girl. Particularly if her mother was problematic.'

'Oh, for God's sake,' I said. 'I wanted to kill my mother and marry my father? That's so trite.'

'I normally try to avoid using terms like "oedipal,"' Dr Silverman said. 'It is merely a label, and as such is not very useful.'

'Then why the hell are we talking about it?'

Dr Silverman smiled and didn't answer.

'Because I introduced the damn term,' I said.

'I think you did,' Dr Silverman said.

24

I had just cleaned up after breakfast with Sarah when the phone rang.

'Sunny Randall?' a voice said.

'Yes.'

It was a whispery voice, as if someone wanted to disguise it.

'I got information about that Sarah Markham case you're working on.'

'Would you like to give it to me?' I said.

'You know the Middlesex Fells?'

'I do.'

'Road runs along the south edge of the woods?' the voice said. 'West of Route Ninety-three?'

'Border Road,' I said.

'Drive there and park anywhere on Border Road. We'll find you.'

'When?'

'When can you get there?' the whispery voice said.

'Noon,' I said.

'Noon,' the voice whispered, and they hung up.

It was 8:30. They were generous with their lead time. Which is dumb. Or amateurish. Or both. I called Spike.

'I need you to be in the woods off Border Road in the Middlesex Fells by eleven a.m. at the latest.'

'Sure,' Spike said. 'Gun or no gun.'

'Gun,' I said.

'Okay,' Spike said, 'tell me about it.'

I told him.

'Ah,' Spike said. 'Movement of some sort. Could it be a feint, and they are after the girl?'

'The thought occurred,' I said. 'I'm making an arrangement.'

'Okay,' Spike said. 'I'll be there.'

'Don't forget your cell phone.'

'Or my gun,' Spike said. 'Or my head.'

I hung up and dialed again and got Tony Marcus.

'Sunny Randall,' he said. 'Always a pleasure.'

'I need a favor.'

'That's what I'm here for,' Tony said. 'Doing favors for Sunny Randall.'

'I need someone to babysit my dog, Rosie...'

'That funny-looking little one with the nose?'

'The beautiful little one with the classic features,' I said, 'and a young, scared white woman who is hiding in my apartment.'

'And why was it I would do that?' Tony said.

'Because you like me,' I said. 'You've told me that often.'

'I do like you, Sunny Randall, except sometimes when you're annoying me.'

'It's only a couple of hours,' I said. 'I'll owe you.'

'That's important,' Tony Marcus said. 'What the hell can you do to pay off a debt to me?'

'Don't be picky,' I said.

Tony gave a deep, soft laugh.

'Can't send you Junior and Ty-Bop,' he said. 'They doing something with me.'

'I don't want to know,' I said.

'No, you don't,' Tony said. 'Send you a guy named Leonard.'

'Is he any good?'

''Course he good,' Tony said. 'Nobody work for me ain't good.'

'Does he like dogs?'

'Leonard don't much like anything,' Tony said. 'One reason he good.'

'But he'll be courteous to both.'

'The dog and the white girl? Yes.'

'I need him now,' I said.

'Here he come,' Tony said. 'You still wired with the Burkes?'

'No.'

'What about Richie?'

'He got married.'

There was silence on the line for a moment.

Then Tony said, 'Oh, well. Can't hurt to have Phil Randall's daughter owe me something.'

'My father's retired,' I said.

'You trying to talk me out of this?' Tony said.

'No. I need the help.'

'He be ringing your doorbell in about five more minutes,' Tony said.

25

Leonard was very black, with good cheekbones. He had on a pinstripe suit and a white shirt with a pin collar and a white silk tie. His head was shaved. He wore a moustache and goatee, and he smelled of very good cologne.

I had already explained Leonard to Sarah. She looked sort of titillated when I introduced them. Rosie came over and smelled his ankle. Leonard looked down at Rosie with no expression at all. Then he went over to the breakfast table and sat.

'Coffee?' he said.

'Fresh pot,' I said. 'Sarah will pour you some.'

He nodded. Sarah got the coffee. I crouched down to kiss Rosie goodbye. Then I stood and got my bag, and checked. Car keys? Gun? Cell phone? Oakleys?

'Nobody in or out,' I said to Leonard. 'I'll be back in a couple of hours.'

'What if you're not?' Sarah said.

'Leonard will stay with you until I am.'

'But, I mean, what if something happens?' she said.

I scribbled *Phil Randall* and a phone number on the blackboard.

'My father,' I said. 'He used to be a cop. He'll know what to do.'

Leonard was drinking coffee out of one of my big, white diner-style mugs. He held the mug softly in both hands.

'Do you have a gun?' Sarah said to him.

Looking at her over the rim of the mug, Leonard nodded.

'Don't answer my phone,' I said.

I smiled at Rosie and said, 'Bye-bye,' and went out the front door and down the steps to my car.

26

At five minutes past eleven, I was driving on South Border Road through thick woods in the Middlesex Fells Reservation. The reservation was probably ten miles from downtown Boston, but it felt like the Canadian Rockies driving through it.

I dialed Spike's cell phone.

When he answered, I said, 'I'm in the woods, driving west.'

'Keep coming,' Spike said. 'I'm about a half mile in.'

'Where's your car?'

'I parked up at the dog meadow and walked down.'

'Seen anybody else?'

'Nope.'

'See me yet?'

'Did you hear me shriek with delight?' Spike said.

'No.'

'Then I haven't seen you.'

'Do you mind if I breathe quietly into the phone?' I said. 'So you'll know I'm alive.'

'Long as you don't sing,' Spike said.

I drove in silence for another minute or so and then, on the phone, Spike said, 'Shriek.' I slowed down.

'Here?' I said.

'Another ten yards,' Spike said. 'Couple of big boulders on the right kind of leaning on each other. Park there.'

'Here?'

'Perfect.'

I pulled over to the shoulder of the road and stopped.

'Where are you?' I said.

'Right behind the boulders.'

'I'm going to get out of the car,' I said, 'and lean on the fender. If things begin to go badly, you appear in force.'

'Can I do my rebel yell?' Spike said.

'Use your best judgment,' I said.

I closed the cell phone and put it in my purse. I took my gun out of my purse and put it in the right-hand side pocket of my belted camel-hair coat, which I always looked good in. I left my purse on the front seat, adjusted my Oakleys, and got out of the car. I stayed on the driver's side and leaned on the front fender and waited. It was the middle of November and getting cold. I put my hands in my pockets. The trees had reacted variously to fall. Some had bare branches. Some had a few yellow leaves. Some were still leafy and at least partially green. It must have something to do with the kinds of trees. Nothing moved in the woods. No one drove along the road. Some birds chirped. I tried not to keep looking at my watch. I looked at the boulders. They were tilted against each other and deeply sunk into the side of the hill, just as they were, probably, when the last glacier melted and left them there. A squirrel ran sort of spasmodically across the road, the way squirrels do, and scrambled up a tree on the other side. There was some gray-green moss on the boulders, and the pale remnants of some sort of vine that had tried to colonize the boulders, but failed fatally.

A dark maroon Chevy sedan appeared from the other direction, driving slowly. It stopped opposite my car, and the window rolled down. The driver was wearing little sunglasses with wire frames and blue lenses. He looked at my license plates for a moment and then said to me, 'Sunny Randall?'

'Yes.'

'Good,' he said and shut off the motor.

He got out of the driver's side, wearing a belted trench coat. A husky man in a brown leather jacket got out of the passenger side. As he walked across the street, I could see the crude lettering in blue ink along the knuckles of each hand. I couldn't read what it said.

The two men stopped in front of me. The guy with the tattoos had shoulder-length black hair that didn't look very clean. The man with the shades looked like his haircut had cost three hundred dollars. His teeth had been worked on. They gleamed like a new sink.

'Cute shades,' I said.

'You know where Sarah Markham is?' the man with the sunglasses said.

'Absolutely,' I said.

'Where?'

'None of your business,' I said.

'She hire you to investigate her parents?'

'She did.'

'You know she's been told to call off the investigation?'

'I do.'

The man with the tattoos was standing very close to me, looking dead-eyed at me.

'But she didn't,' Mr Shades said.

'No,' I said. 'She didn't.'

'She paying you a lot of money?'

'Not so much,' I said.

'Worth getting hurt for?'

'Who is going to hurt me?' I said.

Shades pointed with his chin.

'He is,' he said.

I suddenly stepped away from them into the middle of the road and took out my gun.

'Hey,' Shades said. 'What's with the piece?'

'Alone in the woods with two strange men?' I said. 'What's a girl to do?'

'I got no problem with guns,' Mr Tattoos said.

'You might,' I said.

'You really got the balls to shoot us?' Shades said.

'Balls, no,' I said. 'Shoot, yes.'

'So now what?' Shades said.

'I'll tell you one thing *what*,' Tattoos said. 'No twat is chasing me off.'

I pointed the gun straight at him, holding it in both hands. Behind him, Spike had come out from behind his boulder and was moving softly down the short slope. Spike was both agile and quiet for somebody his size.

'I believe that was an antifeminist remark,' I said. 'Though dated.'

'Fuck you, lady,' Tattoos said.

'Lady is unacceptably incorrect,' I said. 'It dehumanizes women.'

'Never mind the crap,' Shades said. 'You want something?'

'I want to know who hired you to chase me away.'

Shades laughed.

'Whaddya gonna do, shoot us if we don't tell?'

'That won't be necessary,' Spike said from behind them.

Both men whirled around when he spoke. He was behind my car, leaning his thick forearms on the roof.

'Who the fuck are you?' Shades said.

Spike smiled.

'I am, by popular vote,' Spike said, 'the world's toughest queer.'

'What's that supposed to mean?' Shades said.

Spike smiled.

'Turn around,' I said, 'and put your hands on the roof of the car.'

'Like hell,' Shades said.

Spike walked around the car and took a left handful of Shades's slick hair. Spike never seemed to be moving fast, exactly, but things happened very quickly. He slammed Shades's head against the roof of the car. Shades grunted and sagged. Spike held him up with his left hand and patted him down. I kept the gun on Tattoos. Spike took a little .22 semiautomatic out of Shades's side pocket.

'Cute,' Spike said.

He put the gun in his hip pocket and let go. Shades sagged but didn't go down, steadying himself on the car. His forehead was already starting to swell. Spike looked at Tattoos.

'On the car?' Spike said.

'You're pretty tough, got somebody holding a fucking gun on me.'

'And a twat, at that,' Spike said.

74

'Hey,' I said.

Spike jerked his head toward the car. Tattoos put his hands on the roof and Spike patted him down.

'No gun,' Spike said, and stepped back.

Tattoos wasn't very smart. He'd seen Spike handle Mr Shades. He must have noticed that Spike was much bigger than he was. Maybe he thought it was fat. Or maybe he had some outdated theories about sissy-boys. Whatever prompted him, he put his face into Spike's and spoke.

'She didn't have a piece on me...' Tattoos said.

'Sunny,' Spike said to me. 'Put the gun away.'

I put it in my bag, though I cheated a little. I left the bag open and I rested my hand on the edge of it about an inch from the gun's butt.

'You really a fag?' Tattoos said.

'Yep.'

'I never met a fag could fight.'

'What do the tattoos read?' Spike said. *'Jail punk?'*

Tattoos tried to knee Spike in the crotch. Spike turned his hip and the knee caught him harmlessly on it. Tattoos followed with a quick left hook that Spike brushed away with his forearm. He took a handful of Tattoos's shirt in his left hand. Put his right into Tattoos's crotch and swung him up in the air and brought him down hard, on his back, on the trunk of the car. He stepped away and Tattoos slid groggily off the trunk and onto the ground. He stayed there for a moment, then got to his feet unsteadily.

'Jesus Christ,' he said.

'So who hired you to scare off Sarah Markham?' I said.

Timing is everything.

27

The two men leaned somewhat wearily against the car. Spike stood in front of them and a little to the side, with his hands in his hip pockets. I had zipped up my purse, with my gun in it. Neither of them was dangerous anymore. Shades's name was Lewis Karp. The other one was Sal Brunelli.

'Guy came to see me,' Lewis said.

'What was his name?'

'Didn't say.'

I said, 'Tell me about him.'

'Said he was a lawyer from New York.'

'New York City?'

'Yeah, I guess. Said he got my name from a guy in New York. Said he heard from this guy that I could organize something.'

'You know the guy he got your name from?'

'Didn't say. I figure it's probably a guy I did business with down there. Guy named Rosen. Ike Rosen.'

I had my notebook out and was writing down names.

'You talk to Ike,' Lewis said, 'don't say I told you.'

'Of course,' I said. 'What kind of business are you in?'

'Lawyer.'

Spike snorted.

'I got a law degree,' Lewis said. 'I do criminal law.'

'I'll bet you do,' Spike said.

'Is Ike a lawyer, too?' I said.

'Sure.'

'Address?'

'I don't know. All I got is a phone number.'

'I want it,' I said.

'You aren't going to tell Ike you got it from me?'

'No,' I said.

'It's in my Palm Pilot,' he said.

'Where is it?' Spike said.

'My briefcase. In the car.'

'Stay put,' Spike said.

He went to the car and came back with the Palm Pilot. Lewis got the phone number, and I wrote it down. Standing near Lewis, Spike was rocking slightly back and forth, hands still in his hip pockets. No cars had passed us since we'd been there. The sun had moved a little west. Birds still chirped.

Squirrels still darted haltingly about.

'Don't make stuff up,' Spike said to Lewis.

I said, 'He wouldn't lie to us, Spike.'

'I'm not lying.'

Spike smiled at him and didn't say anything.

'What did the gentleman want?' I said.

'He said could I put together a little something to scare off someone who was annoying his client.'

'Was he a lawyer?'

'I thought he was.'

'Takes one to know one,' Spike said pleasantly to Sal.

Sal didn't look at him. Lewis looked at me.

'So let's not make this twenty questions,' I said. 'Tell me all about it and maybe you can get out of here without Spike stepping on your face.'

'Told me the girl's name. Said he wanted her scared off. Wanted the investigation stopped.'

'He say what investigation?'

'No. He gave me the girl's dorm address and told me to tell her that and rough her up.'

'Did you get paid?'

'Of course,' Lewis said.

'How?'

'Guy gave me five grand. Cash. I give half to Sal and we go do it.'

'So how'd you get to me?' I said.

'Got another visit. Same guy. Said you needed to get the same message. Gimme your license plate numbers, told me to find you.'

'What was I worth?'

'Same thing. Five.'

'You should have charged more,' I said. 'How do I reach you?'

'I got an office in the South End,' he said. 'Warren Street. I work out of my home.'

Spike took a business card from his pocket, and held it up. The card said *Lewis Karp, Attorney at Law,* with an address in Brighton.

'From your briefcase,' Spike said.

'Oh, shit,' Lewis said.

He looked at me.

'Well, hell, I mean, can you blame me not wanting Godzilla' – he nodded at Spike – 'knowing where to find me?'

'You are dumb, even for a lawyer,' I said. 'I have the registration number off your car. Do you think I wouldn't have checked?'

Lewis shrugged.

'I dunno,' he said.

'We're going to continue the investigation,' I said.

Lewis nodded.

'No one is going to bother Sarah Markham again,' I said.

'No.'

'If anyone does – you, Sal, the mystery lawyer, Britney Spears, anyone – it won't matter. We will come looking for you.'

'I can't control...' Lewis started.

'I don't care. Spike doesn't care. Do you, Spikey?'

'I want to visit with you again,' Spike said. 'I like guys that will beat up a twenty-one-year-old girl without even knowing why.'

'If anything happens to her,' I said, 'you are dead.'

Spike opened his coat wide enough so that they could see the big Army .45 he was wearing. Nobody said anything.

'Go,' I said.

The two men went to their car. Sal was walking uncomfortably. Spike and I watched them drive away.

'I'll drive you to your car,' I said.

Spike looked at me as if he was about to say something serious.

'Spikey?' he said.

'I try to remain girlish,' I said.

Spike grinned. 'Me too,' he said.

28

I wanted Spike to meet Sarah for future reference. So after I dropped him off at his car, he followed me back to my loft. I used my key to enter downstairs. But the loft door was bolted and I had to knock. There were quiet footsteps and then silence while Leonard checked us through the peephole.

'Who's with you?' Leonard said from inside.

'My friend Spike, it's okay.'

'What's my name?' Leonard said.

'Leonard.'

The bolt slid back, and the door opened.

'Clever,' I said to Leonard. 'If Spike were the enemy, I could have let you know by saying your name was Arthur or something.'

Leonard nodded.

'You all set now?' he said.

Rosie rushed down the length of the loft, and I crouched to say hello.

'Yes,' I said. 'Thank you, Leonard.'

'Thank Tony,' Leonard said, and left.

Spike looked after him.

'What a fine-looking man,' Spike said.

Rosie did a couple spins and wagged her tail rapidly and made a little squeak. Sarah sat on the couch, smoking. She was staring at Spike.

'Fine,' Spike said.

I stood. Spike bent over and scooped up Rosie and gave her a series of rapid kisses on the nose.

'Everything okay, Sarah?' I said.

'Yeah. It's okay. That guy Leonard doesn't talk much.'

'Might be a good thing,' I said. 'This is Spike.'

'He's the one I'm supposed to call if you're not here.'

'Who you gonna call?' Spike said, and put out his hand.

Sarah took it languidly.

'Girl,' Spike said, 'you have a handshake like a noodle.'

Sarah shrugged.

'We found the men who beat you up,' I said.

'What happened?'

'We spoke to them firmly,' I said. 'And they agreed not to bother you again.'

'You spoke to them?'

'Yes,' I said.

'The tough guy? The one with the tattoos?'

'Yes. His name is Sal Brunelli.'

'What did he do?'

'He bounced,' Spike said.

'What?'

I smiled. 'Spike picked him up and banged him on his car.'

'You picked him up?'

'I did,' Spike said. 'Actually, I've picked up quite a few men in my life.'

I smiled. Sarah stared at Spike. It might have been awe.

'What would you have done?' Sarah said to me.

'Without Spike?'

'Yes. I mean, you're a woman.'

'Hear me shout,' I said. 'I had a gun.'

'Would you have shot them?'

'As needed,' I said.

Sarah was silent. Spike and Rosie had settled on the couch beside her. Rosie was on her back, and Spike was rubbing her stomach. Sarah watched this for a moment, and then looked back at me.

'How can you do this?' she said.

'This?' I said.

'Be a detective and face bad guys and stuff... and you need a man to protect you.'

'Good heavens,' Spike said to Rosie. 'A feminist conundrum.'

There was coffee left. I poured some.

'It's good to know your limitations,' I said. 'I weigh one hundred twenty-six pounds. Sal Brunelli, tattoos and all, weighs... what, Spike? You picked him up?'

'A hundred ninety-two and a half,' Spike said.

'That's a significant disparity,' I said to Sarah, 'but a common one. Most men are bigger and stronger than I am. So I need an equalizer.'

I put my coffee down and got my purse and opened it and took out the short-barreled .38 I carried.

'This is one,' I said.

Sarah stared at the gun. I put the gun back and walked over to Spike and touched his shoulder.

'And this is another. One reason I sometimes prefer Spike is that his, ah, equalizing capacity can be modulated. The gun tends to be pretty black-and-white.'

'You brought Spike with you so you wouldn't have to shoot them?'

'Think of it this way,' Spike said. 'I wasn't there to protect her from them. I was there to protect them from her.'

'Did you have a gun, too?'

'Yes,' Spike said. 'Most people I meet are not bigger and stronger than I am. But they might have an equalizer, too.'

Sarah was drinking her coffee black and was lighting one cigarette from the butt of the other.

'Did they have guns?' she said.

'The lawyer-y guy, Lewis Karp – who was, by the way, a lawyer, nice call.'

'He had one?'

'Yes.' Spike reached into his coat pocket and held it up.

'It's small,' she said.

'Big enough,' I said.

Sarah was silent for a time. Tears began to well.

'People with guns,' she said. 'I have people with guns in my life, and people beating me up, and all I'm trying to do is find out who I am.'

'I think you can go back to school,' I said. 'I'll drive you there, and I'll talk with campus security. No one will bother you.'

'For how long?'

'Long enough for me to find out who you are.'

'You believe me? That those people aren't my parents?'

'I believe that something is quite wrong in your family,' I said.

29

I called the number Karp had given me for Ike Rosen. Answering machine. I called Information. There were about seventy-five Isaac Rosens. I gave them the phone number and asked for an address. The number was unlisted. They couldn't give me an address. I called my father.

'Can you get me the address,' I said, 'if I give you the phone number?'

'Of course.'

'Wow,' I said, 'even though you're retired.'

'I'm retired, not dead,' my father said. 'I'll call you back.'

It took him five minutes. When the phone rang again, I picked it up and said, 'Is this the great Phil Randall?'

'The man and the legend,' my father said. 'Your man Ike Rosen lives and, I assume, works on West Ninety-second Street.'

He gave me the address.

'Same phone number?' I said.

'Yes. He's listed as an attorney.'

'Any other phone numbers?'

'No.'

'Thanks, Daddy.'

'Captain Daddy,' my father said.

'Yes, sir.'

After I hung up, I called Rosen again. Same answering machine. I didn't leave a message. I couldn't think how to rephrase, 'Did you arrange to have me beaten up?' Rosie was asleep on my bed, between two pillows, so all you could see were her back feet sticking out. It was almost five o'clock in the afternoon. I went and got a bottle of white wine from the refrigerator and brought it with a glass to the breakfast table. I poured some and had a sip. Everything was so quiet that I could hear my wind-up alarm clock ticking by my bed near the other end of the loft. Outside, it was raining, and I looked out my window for a time and drank my wine and watched it.

How did I know Daddy liked me best? Why wouldn't he? His wife was a bossy nitwit. His older daughter was a snobby nitwit. He and I understood things. We knew what mattered and what didn't. My marriage had failed. But only once. Elizabeth was on her third husband. And Daddy still loved her. And he loved my mother. In fact, the way he loved her made me think maybe love was irrational. Simply a force that happened to you, like gravity. She was so unworthy of his affection. Maybe he actually didn't love me best. Maybe he just liked me best. And even if he did love me more than he loved my mother, what was wrong with that? I was more lovable. Why would that be such a burden? Granted, she had the advantage of sleeping with him...

Oh.

That's why. All my life, the three Randall girls had been fighting for Phil's affections. Sometimes it seemed as if I'd won. But what if I really won?

Sex.

There's your heavy burden, Sonya. (I always used my real name when I talked to myself.) Everybody since Sophocles knew that was trouble. I poured some more wine. There was no wind. The rain was unhurried as it fell. And clean. So even if it was in some subconscious, symbolic way the fear that I might actually win the fight for Daddy... what did that do to Richie and me?

I stood and carried my wine glass down to the window at the other end of the loft and looked at the rain from there. I felt like crying. I was breathing hard. A few tears formed and wet my face.

'Well, Sonya,' I said out loud, 'there'll be something to talk about with Dr Susan next time.' I felt a little guilty. I would never call her Dr Susan to her face. *Rebellion, I guess.*

30

Ike Rosen's home and office was in a nice-looking brownstone on 92nd Street just west of Broadway. I didn't know what he looked like, so I rang his bell every time a man entered the building. At a quarter to twelve, I rang the super's bell. He came to the front door and talked to me outside on the top step.

'I'm with Lexington Insurance Company,' I said. 'I have a claim settlement check for someone named Isaac Rosen at this address.'

'You want me to hold it?' the super said.

'Can't,' I said. 'I have to hand it to him. And I have to get his signature. Do you know where he is?'

'Probably out chasing ambulances,' the super said. 'Nice-looking babe like you. You shouldn't be hustling insurance payments.'

'Gotta work,' I said. 'Can you tell me what Mr Rosen looks like?'

'You don't have to work,' the super said. He had thick black eyebrows and receding hair. His green work shirt was buttoned to the neck. 'You should have a sugar daddy.'

'It's hard to find one I like,' I said.

The super thought about that for a minute. Then he nodded.

'Yeah, you right. Never thought about liking them.'

'Rosen?' I said.

'Fat guy. Short. Red face. Hair's kind of thin. Always wears double-breasted suit, you know. Very natty. Suits always dark.'

'Is he fat, fat?' I said.

'Fat, fat, fat,' the super said.

'Thanks,' I said.

'I see him, I tell him you looking,' he said.

I nodded and went back down the stairs and across the street. At 1:45, a very fat man in a dark blue double-breasted suit came down the street, eating some sort of drippy sandwich. He walked leaning forward so whatever was leaking out of the sandwich wouldn't get on his shirt front. Given his size, the suit fit him well. With it, he was wearing a starched white shirt with a Windsor collar and a pale blue silk tie. A white silk handkerchief spilled dashingly out of his breast pocket.

'Mr Rosen?' I said.

'Well, well,' he said. 'My day's looking up.'

'I'd like to talk with you, if I may.'

'Looking way up,' Rosen said. 'My place or yours.'

He had longish white hair. His pink face was clean-shaven and healthy-looking. He smelled of cologne, and maybe a little of bourbon. His hands were small, and he wore a diamond pinkie ring. His feet, in wingtipped black tasseled loafers, looked too small for him.

'We could sit right on your front steps,' I said, 'and talk while you finish your sandwich.'

'We could,' he said. 'Or we could go up to my place and talk, over a couple of drinks.'

I smiled at him.

'The steps are fine,' I said.

He shrugged. I tucked my skirt under me and sat on the top steps of the brownstone. He sat beside me. He had no trouble getting down. Except that he was fat, he didn't seem fat. He leaned forward and carefully took another bite of his sandwich.

'Pork barbecue,' he said. 'Saloon on the corner sells it.'

'It looks good,' I said.

'Happy to take you up there and buy you some,' Rosen said.

'No thanks,' I said. 'Do you know Lewis Karp?'

'Karp?'

'In Boston,' I said.

'Lew Karp,' he said as if he were thinking.

'The answer is yes,' I said. 'I know you know him.'

'Then why did you ask?'

'Standard investigative procedure.'

'You a cop?'

'Not anymore,' I said. 'You sent an attorney to see him.'

He was looking at my knees. The hem had slipped back a little. I made no effort to adjust it. In certain circumstances, that was also standard investigative procedure.

'You used to be a cop,' he said. 'What are you now? Insurance? Private?'

'Private,' I said.

He finished his sandwich and wiped his mouth and hands carefully on a napkin, which he then dropped to the sidewalk. He leaned over and patted my bare knee.

He said, 'How much you want the information, hon?'

'So there is information?' I said.

'There might be,' he said. 'Lemme make a suggestion. We go upstairs to my place. I break out a bottle of Jack Daniel's. We have a couple over ice. We talk. We see what develops. Huh?'

I thought about it. How much was I willing to let him paw me to find out what I wanted to know? Not much. But he didn't have to know that until the pawing started. I tried to look titillated.

'Well, you certainly are direct,' I said.

He stood and carefully shook his cuffs down over his shoe tops.

'Life's too short,' he said. 'Let's continue this upstairs.'

'I guess that would be okay,' I said.

He smiled at me and unlocked the front door.

He lived one flight up in a small, very neat apartment, which smelled equally of cologne and bourbon. I sat on a straight chair next to the fireplace, with my knees together and my purse in my lap, while he made me a drink. I was working on a prim but excited demeanor. He handed me the drink and went and sat on the sofa. The drink was in a nice, thick lowball glass.

'Come on over here,' he said. 'Easier to talk if we're side by side, don't you think?'

'I really need to know that lawyer's name,' I said.

He looked at my knees some more, and touched his lower lip with the tip of his tongue. I was wearing my camel's hair coat, which was unbuttoned.

'We can talk about him in a while,' he said. 'Drink a little of that Jack Daniel's. Good Tennessee whiskey.'

I pretended to sip. I wasn't much of a bourbon drinker, and

I also had no way to know what else was in the drink.

'That's the way,' he said. 'Come on over here.'

I smiled.

'If you expect me to show you mine,' I said, 'you've got to show me yours.'

'Show you... ?'

'Who was the lawyer you sent to see Lewis Karp?'

'I tell you and you'll come sit beside me?'

I smiled and tried to bat my eyes. I think I just blinked them.

'You won't have to go all the way,' he said. 'We could, you know, just do a little touching.'

He drank half his bourbon.

'That doesn't sound too bad,' I said.

He grinned.

'I don't have to get on top of you or anything. I know I'd crush you.'

'Touching sounds nice,' I said.

He grinned and patted the couch beside him.

'Sit here, baby.'

'So, who was that lawyer?' I said.

'Oh, hell,' he said. 'Pete Franklin.'

'Short for Peter?'

'Peter Winslow Franklin. Come on and sit down now.'

'And what if we, you know, do whatever, and I find out afterwards you were lying?'

'Jesus Christ,' he said.

He took a long, slim wallet out of his inside coat pocket, and opened it and took out a business card, and held it out to me. I leaned forward and took it and read it. It read *Peter W. Franklin,* and the firm's name: Harrop and Moriarty. And a midtown Manhattan address.

'Here's his damn card. Now come over here and put that cute ass down beside mine and let's get things going.'

I put the card in my side pocket and stood.

'Thanks for the drink,' I said.

'What the fuck are you doing?' he said.

'I strung you along,' I said. 'I'm sorry.'

'You fucking bitch,' he said.

He stood and moved in front of the apartment door.

'You lying fucking bitch,' he said.

I almost felt bad for him.

'I'm going now,' I said.

'The fuck you are,' he said. 'We had a deal.'

'Step out of the way,' I said.

I still had the drink in my left hand.

'You ain't leaving, without you doing a few things like you promised.'

I sighed. There was no reason to mess with it. I threw my drink, glass and all, into his face. The rim of the glass caught him on the bridge of the nose and drew blood. He turned his head away and tried to wipe the bourbon out of his eyes, and I took a leather sap out of my right-hand coat pocket and hit him hard behind the left knee. It made the knee buckle, and he fell sideways. He started to cry.

'Bitches, you're all bitches, all of you, bitch…'

I stepped past him and opened the door and went on down the stairs to the street. I felt kind of bad.

31

Harrop and Moriarty had offices on 57th across from Carnegie Hall, in the penthouse. There was a security guard in the lobby of the building, and the Harrop and Moriarty receptionist had to buzz the door open when I rang the bell. She was sleek and blonde and probably twenty-two. She was wearing a headset and microphone, and she spoke into the microphone and pushed some buttons several times while I stood.

'Harrop and Moriarty,' she said. 'One moment, please.'

Pushed a button.

'Harrop and Moriarty. One moment, please.'

Pushed a button.

Finally, she looked up at me and smiled automatically.

'Peter Franklin,' I said.

'Do you have an appointment?'

'My name is Randall,' I said. 'About Ike Rosen and Sarah Markham.'

She continued to smile.

'And did you have an appointment?'

'Ask Mr Franklin,' I said. 'He'll want to see me.'

The receptionist sighed an understated I've-been-there-and-heard-that sigh, and punched a button.

'Ms Randall, sir, about Ike Rosen and Sarah Markham.'

She listened for a minute and punched a button.

'Mr Franklin will be right out to get you, Ms Randall,' the receptionist said.

If she was disappointed, she didn't show it. Very professional.

I stood for a moment, and a very handsome young man came down the corridor toward me. His dark hair was short and looked as if it never needed to be combed or cut. He wore a dark brown Harris tweed jacket and a tattersall shirt with a black knit tie. His charcoal flannel slacks were creased; his dark burgundy brogues gleamed with polish. When he put out a hand to me, I could see that his nails were manicured.

'Ms Randall? Peter Franklin.'

His handshake was strong and square. He looked me straight in the eye when he spoke. His teeth gleamed evenly. His cologne was subtle. He was only a little taller than I was, but it was a minor flaw. Overall, he was spectacular.

'Let's go on down to my office,' he said.

He was obviously a firm favorite. His office had two windows. I sat in a comfortable client chair with stainless-steel arms. He went behind his glass-topped stainless-steel semicircular desk and sat in his stainless-steel designer swivel chair. There was a big-screen television set and an assortment of VCR and DVD players wired into it, all in a big stainless-steel cabinet. I sensed a decorative theme. There were pictures galleried on the wall opposite his desk. Each had a stainless-steel frame. I nodded at the pictures.

'Clients?' I said.

'Yes,' Franklin said. 'I work almost exclusively in the talent-representation end of the business.'

He put his palms together as if he was going to pray and pressed his fingertips against his lips and gazed at me.

'What is your first name, Ms Randall?'

'Legally,' I said, 'It's Sonya, but I prefer Sunny.'

'Sunny Randall,' he said.

'Yes.'

'Wasn't there a football player?'

'My father's little joke,' I said. 'I spell mine S-u-n-n-y.'

He smiled, and his hazel eyes bored sincerely into mine.

'I spell mine P-e-t-e,' he said. 'What brings you to me, Sunny?'

'Ike Rosen and Sarah Markham,' I said.

He frowned a little.

'Rosen, I know,' he said. 'Worked here once for a little while. Heard he was disbarred.'

'So the phrase "attorney at law" on his card is misleading?' I said.

'He cannot practice law in the state of New York,' Peter said. 'Sarah I don't know.'

'Sarah Markham,' I said.

Peter thought and thought and finally shook his head sadly.

'No, I simply don't know Sarah Markham,' he said.

'How about Lewis Karp?' I said.

Peter looked bemused.

'Am I on *Candid Camera*?' he said. 'What are you up to, Sunny?'

I took one of my cards out of my purse and handed it to him. He read it and sat back.

'Aha,' he said. 'Well, you are about the best-looking detective I know.'

'Yes, thank you, I probably am,' I said. 'Tell me about Lewis Karp and Ike Rosen.'

'I can tell you about Rosen,' Peter said. 'He is a drunk and a compulsive liar. We fired him here.'

'What was he disbarred for?' I said.

'I don't know the details. Some sort of financial irregularities. It was after he'd left us.'

'He says he put you in touch with a lawyer in Boston named Lewis Karp,' I said.

Peter smiled broadly.

'Ike Rosen? If I need a contact in Boston I can get one without Ike Rosen. Usually, we do business with Cone Oakes.'

'Good firm,' I said. 'But according to Lew Karp, you needed someone who could arrange to have Sarah Markham beaten up. Cone Oakes might not have been your best bet.'

Peter took his praying hands down from his lips and clasped them on the desk before him and leaned toward me. Sincerity radiated from him like strong aftershave.

'I don't know Sarah Markham. I don't know Lew Karp. I don't want anyone beaten up.' He smiled at me. 'Except maybe all of the Knicks. I represent some of the most important media people in the country. I don't arrange beatings.'

'So Rosen's lying and Karp's lying?'

'I don't know Karp. I don't know what he's doing. Rosen is lying.'

'Did you have a hand in firing Rosen?' I said.

'I was on the review committee,' he said.

'Maybe it's revenge,' I said.

'Maybe.'

Peter looked at his Rolex.

'Damn,' he said. 'Sunny, I'm stalling a record producer to talk with you. I really have to get to him.'

'Of course,' I said. 'If I need anything more I'll call you.'

'I can do better than that. Why don't I meet you after work at the bar in the Four Seasons restaurant and buy you a drink?'

'I'd love that,' I said.

'About, say, six-fifteen?'

'Perfect,' I said. 'That's the restaurant not the hotel.'

'Yes.'

'Fifty-second Street,' I said. 'Between Park and Lex.'

'Exactly.'

'Six-fifteen,' I said, and stood up.

He stood. We shook hands. He gave mine a little squeeze. Our eyes met. He smiled. I smiled. This could be the start of something big. The only thing was, I thought as I went down in the elevator, that the first picture in the top row of his client gallery was Lolly Drake, the big-star talk-show woman who had started in Moline with George Markham more than twenty years ago.

That was bothersome.

32

Sitting at the bar in the Four Seasons Grill Room under the several-story ceiling, sipping a martini made with Grey Goose L'Orange vodka, I was on my first date since Richie got married. Unless you counted Ike Rosen. Granted, it was a working date. It was still a date. The room was full of well-dressed people who looked successful in that New York way, including my date.

'So how did a beautiful woman like you,' he said, 'turn out to be a detective?'

I had hoped for a more original opener. But he had said *beautiful*.

'I was an art major in college,' I said.

'Art history?'

'No,' I said. 'I paint.'

'Wow,' Peter said. 'I'd love to see some of your work.'

He was drinking Glenfiddich on the rocks in a squat, manly glass.

'I hope you will,' I said.

'So, how's that segue to detective work?' he said.

'I needed to earn a living until my paintings began to sell,' I said. 'And my father was a cop. I like the work. It's interesting. Sometimes I'm helpful to people. And I get to set my own hours.'

'You live alone?' he said.

'I live with Rosie, the world's most beautiful bull terrier.'

'Being the world's most beautiful bull terrier,' Peter said, 'is not necessarily a challenge.'

I stared at him without speaking. He looked at me and smiled.

'She must be very beautiful,' he said. 'I gather you're not married.'

'Divorced,' I said.

He nodded as if to say, 'Aren't we all?'

'Anyone in your life right now?' he said.

'Right now?' I said. 'You.'

'Well, aren't you literal?' he said.

I smiled. 'So why did you decide to see me?' I said.

'I had a premonition,' he said.

'The names I mentioned didn't count?'

'Well, hell,' he said, and sipped his scotch. 'I knew Ike Rosen, at least.'

'The receptionist didn't expect you to see me.'

'Just that feeling,' he said.

He gave me a little toast with his glass.

'You know… this could be the start of something big.'

'And you never heard of Lewis Karp?'

'Must you keep carping on him?'

I smiled.

'That's awful,' I said.

He nodded.

'Awful,' he said.

'You represent Lolly Drake?'

'I do,' he said. 'And Andy Wescott – you know, the star of that cop show. And Chuck Wells, the news anchor.' He smiled. 'Lawyer to the stars,' he said.

'What's she like?' I said.

'Lolly?'

I nodded.

'Just what you see and hear,' he said. 'Smart, tough woman. Sees clearly, thinks clearly. And a knockout to boot.'

'Do you know where she started?' I said.

'Oh, hell, East Overshoe, someplace. I don't know. The

Midwest. Some rinky-dink eight-watt radio station. She was their' – he made quote marks in the air and lowered his voice – 'law correspondent.'

'And it built from there?'

'Yeah. It became a "call-in, ask Lolly" kind of program, and then the subject matter broadened' – he waved his hand – 'the rest is history.

'The firm has represented her since she went national,' he said. 'I took her on personally, I'd say, about ten years ago.'

'She fun to work with?'

'You bet,' he said. 'You always know where you stand with Lolly.'

'But is she fun?' I said.

'Probably not as much fun as you. Why the interest?'

'Hell,' I said. 'What woman wouldn't be interested? She's a hero to us all.'

'I can see why she would be,' Peter said.

'Do you do all her legal work?'

'We do everything,' Peter said. 'Legal, representation, the whole deal.'

'I'd love to meet her,' I said.

Peter tilted his head.

'Might be possible,' he said. 'Would you like dinner here, or would you like to come back to my place?'

'Do you cook?' I said.

'Elegantly,' he said.

'And would there be something really good for dessert?' I said.

He smiled at me and let the question hang for a moment.

Then he said, 'I guess that would be pretty much up to you.'

It was possible that Peter would turn out to be the enemy. I was alone in New York. My ex-husband had remarried.

'Let's find out,' I said.

33

The red digital display on the cable box in Peter's bedroom said that it was 2:30 in the morning. I was lying on my back beside Peter, listening to him snore softly. I had no clothes on. I wished very much to be dressed and in a cab back to my hotel. I wished I were back in my hotel, dressed in an oversized two-tone-orange T-shirt, and in my bed. Like so many liberated, up-to-the-minute contemporary men I had met, Peter felt it was important to spend the night together. No slam, bam, thank you, ma'am. Which meant a sort of awkward maneuvering around the bathroom in the morning. It meant wriggling into my pantyhose while he watched. Or it meant picking up my clothes and getting dressed in the closet.

Ick!

There was no real basis for speculating about Lolly Drake. Except the coincidence that she knew Sarah's father. And she was represented by a man who may have hired someone to beat up Sarah. But if I decided that it was a meaningless coincidence, and that Ike Rosen had probably lied to me, in the grip of his passion, then I had nowhere to go, and the discovery of that coincidence did nothing for me. And if it wasn't a coincidence, I might be sleeping with the enemy. I decided to assume that it wasn't a coincidence. So what if I had slept with the enemy.

The red-letter clock told me it was ten of three. I slipped out of bed and tiptoed to the chair where my clothes were folded and got dressed in careful silence. The pantyhose seemed too challenging at three in the morning, so I put them in my handbag and, carrying my shoes, I tiptoed out of the bedroom and through the living room, where the ambient light of the city showed the empty champagne bottle and two fluted glasses standing in mute memory of our evening. I stepped into my shoes while the elevator dropped silently to the lobby.

There was a sleepy doorman at the desk. I smiled at him demurely, trying not to look like a floozy, as I went by him and out onto Fifth Avenue. There is very little emptier than anywhere at three in the morning. I didn't see a cab. The night was pleasant enough, so I headed downtown and walked twenty-one blocks down Fifth to my hotel. Most of the way, Central Park was on my right: lovely, dark, and deep. And beyond it, the eternal lights of the West Side marked its westward definition.

At my hotel, I had to ring to get in. I tried my I'm-not-a-floozy look on the security man who checked my room key. It's a hard look to pull off when you are coming home alone at three in the morning with your pantyhose in your purse. I'm not sure he bought it.

Upstairs, I brushed my teeth and took a long shower and put on my orange T-shirt and went to bed and fell asleep almost as soon as I was prone. I dreamed Rosie and I were walking in a landscape I'd never seen, and Rosie was running around in ever-widening circles. When I called her, she came back, but then as we walked, she would continue to stray farther and farther until I called her back.

In the morning, I awoke with no new insights about myself or Peter Franklin, but I felt rested and lay in bed for a while being alone, reading the room-service menu, thinking about breakfast. Love and sex were great. Especially when they overlapped. But alone had its moments, too.

Two hours later, freshly showered, with a fine breakfast settling comfortably and my teeth newly brushed, I left the hotel and went to work.

It was 11:20, bright and cold with some wind coming up 57th Street off the Hudson, when I settled in opposite Peter Franklin's office. I was in jeans and sneakers and a warm black trench coat with a lot of zippers. I had on a dark wool watch cap, pulled down over my ears, the kind of hat that I would have to wear for the rest of the day, or suffer the heartbreak of hat hair. In my coat pocket I had a little digital camera with a zoom on it. I looked at my watch. I was betting he'd come out for lunch in the next hour or two.

I had checked out of my hotel. My luggage was in my car, and my car was parked in a garage near Tenth Avenue. Get my pictures and beat it north along the Hudson. While I had been lolling around my room, enjoying solitude and eating breakfast, the phone had rung three times. Each time, I didn't answer. Each time my message light began to flash, and when I checked the voice mail it was Peter Franklin.

The first message was, 'Hey, babe. Where'd you go? Was it something I did... or something I didn't do? I want to see you again. Give me a call.'

The second and third messages were variations of the first. The second message also contained a graphic anatomical compliment.

Oh, shucks.

The size and quickness of New York always excited me. It always made me think of the way Lewis Mumford had defined a city. Something like 'the most options in the least space.' It was all of that.

I was comfortable in New York. I had lived all my life only four hours up the road, and was pretty much at home in Manhattan, though, like most people who didn't live in New York City, I had only limited experience of the Bronx, Queens, and Brooklyn, and was pretty sure I'd never even been to Staten Island.

I wasn't much worried that Peter would see me. He wasn't expecting to see me. I had on the hat and big sunglasses, and was dressed very differently from the last time he'd seen me, even not counting the time he'd seen me undressed. Even if he did see me, it wouldn't matter much. I'd say I was on my way to say goodbye and stopped to take a sentimental-memory picture of his office building.

At one o'clock I bought a soft pretzel from a vendor and ate it. With yellow mustard. At 1:15, Peter appeared in the doorway of his building with two other men. All three wore dark overcoats and light scarves. Peter had on a soft hat with a wide brim like crime bosses wear in movies. The three of them stopped to talk for a moment on the sidewalk outside the building, and I took some pictures. Peter was animated. The two men nodded. Then one of them talked with a lot of hand gestures, and Peter kept shaking his head. Then, finally, he put his hand up and the man who had been gesturing gave him a high-five and the three of them laughed. The two men turned west and walked away. Peter stood, looking after them, ever solicitous, and I took some more pictures. Then he turned and walked east, toward Sixth Avenue. I put my camera away and headed for my car, walking straight into the wind with my head down a little to keep it from blowing grit in my face.

34

Dr Silverman was wearing a black suit and a white silk top. She had pearls around her neck and quiet pearl earrings. As usual, she wore no rings. Many married women, of course, didn't wear wedding rings. I hadn't worn one much when I was married. Richie had. He wore his like an amulet or something. I wondered if that was meaningful.

'Here's what happened on my trip to New York,' I said.

Dr Silverman raised her eyebrows a little to let me know that she was fascinated.

'You know the case I'm working on, Sarah Markham's real parents and such?'

Dr Silverman nodded. *Did she really remember or was she just encouraging me?*

'Well, after Spike and I had the confrontation with the two guys in the woods...'

I looked at her to make sure she remembered. I knew she had many patients. I knew she didn't take notes. I couldn't believe she recorded the sessions without my knowledge. So I was dependent on her memory.

'Spike is a useful friend,' she said.

Apparently, she remembered. Though she was so nondirective, as she always was, that I couldn't be sure. I gave it up.

'Anyway,' I said. 'They gave me a name, a lawyer named Ike Rosen, and I went to New York and Ike gave me a name, a lawyer named Peter Franklin, and I talked with Franklin, and he turns out to represent Lolly Drake, the talk-show lady?'

Dr Silverman nodded.

'And Lolly Drake started her career at the same station, at the same time, that George Markham was there.'

'It could be a coincidence,' Dr Silverman said.

'It could be,' I said. 'But deciding that it is leads me nowhere... deciding that it isn't presents an opportunity.'

'That's true,' Dr Silverman said.

Her hands looked strong. Her nails were perfectly manicured with a clear polish that made them gleam quietly. It was hard to figure how old she was. Older than I.

'The thing is,' I said. 'Sex reared its ugly head.'

'Ugly?' Dr Silverman said.

'It's just, you know, a phrase,' I said.

Dr Silverman nodded.

'Tell me about it,' she said.

So I told her about letting Rosen think I'd sleep with him, and I told her about sleeping with Franklin.

'I took some pictures of him,' I said. 'I'll show them to Karp and see if Franklin is the man who hired him.'

'And if he is?'

'I've been sleeping with the enemy.'

'A possibility you knew about when you chose to,' Dr Silverman said.

'Yes.'

Dr Silverman was quiet.

'I feel kind of dirty,' I said.

'How so?'

'Well, pretending I'd, ah, come across for poor, fat Ike Rosen, just so I could get him to tell me what I needed to know.'

'You're in a tough business,' Dr Silverman said. 'There's no reason not to use whatever advantages you have.'

'I suppose.'

'Do you feel dirty about Franklin?' Dr Silverman said.

'No. Isn't that odd?'

'Odd?'

'Yes. I mean, he may be a very bad man, and I knew he might be, and I hopped right into bed with him.'

'His faults may be his charm,' Dr Silverman said.

'What's that mean?' I said.

'Perhaps you can enjoy him more,' she said, 'because he's almost certainly not going to become a long-term relationship.'

'Because he might be a bad guy?'

'You didn't spend the night,' Dr Silverman said.

'No,' I said. 'I hate to spend the night.'

'Really?'

'You know… how you look when you wake up and how he does, and the bathroom business, and getting dressed while he watches you… It's all just, sort of, ah, uncomfortable, once the passion subsides. Besides, he might want to again, and I never want to first thing in the morning.'

Dr Silverman smiled. I wondered if she ever worried about spending the night.

'Do you think leaving when the sex is over underscores that it's only about sex?'

'I suppose,' I said.

We were quiet. Dr Silverman watched me pleasantly. I drummed my fingers gently on my thighs for a moment. Dr Silverman watched me do that. A student of body language, too? It was very interesting, what we'd talked about. Did I want to make it clear that it was in fact only slam, bam, thank you, ma'am? Or was it after all only the inconveniences of spending the night with anyone you didn't know well… or did?

I said, 'Let me tell you about a dream.'

She nodded.

'I'm out walking in a rural landscape with Rosie. There's a little arched bridge over a stream at the top of a hill where we're walking. It's not a place I've been to in real life, that I can remember. It's sort of a generic painterly kind of still-life landscape. Rosie keeps running in wider and wider circles.

When I call her, she comes back, but not all the way. She's having a grand time. But I'm a little uneasy about her running loose without any certainty that she'll come back. Usually, she's on a leash.'

Dr Silverman waited. Still interested.

'And that's all,' I said.

'How did you feel?'

'In the dream or when I woke up?'

Dr Silverman smiled.

'Either one,' she said.

'In the dream, as I said, I was uneasy, anxious about her.'

Dr Silverman nodded.

'And after?' she said. 'When you were awake?'

'That's the funny thing,' I said. 'Now, awake, I kind of like the dream. I like to think about her running free like that.'

'Unleashed,' Dr Silverman said.

I looked at her for a moment. What was she up to?

'Yes,' I said. 'Unleashed.'

She nodded and was quiet. I was quiet. I didn't know where to go with it. After a while, Dr Silverman looked at her watch. She always did it the same way. It was ritualized. A way to say, 'It's time.'

'I...'

'We're out of time today,' she said.

'I don't...'

She waited a minute.

Then she said, 'There's no hurry. I'll see you Thursday.'

I stood and walked to the door. She stood as she always did and walked to the door with me.

'Unleashed,' I said.

She smiled and opened the door.

I went out.

35

Under the heading of no hard feelings, I had lunch with Lewis Karp, at a coffee shop on Washington Street in Brighton. Lewis looked around a bit nervously when he came in, and didn't see Spike, and seemed to relax. He ordered a cheeseburger. I had tuna salad on whole wheat. We both had coffee.

'So, you talk to Ike Rosen?' Karp said.

The continuing absence of Spike seemed to make him positively expansive.

'I did.'

'He's a great guy, isn't he?'

'A very friendly person,' I said.

'So, did he help you out?'

'Yes. He sent me to a lawyer named Peter Franklin,' I said.

'And?'

I took an eight-by-ten blowup out of my big shoulder bag and handed it to Karp. He studied it, making a considerable show of frowning and turning the picture for a different angle.

'I think that might be him,' Karp said. 'You got any other shots?'

I took several more out of my bag and placed them side by side on the table. Karp looked some more. Frowning, squinting, sitting back, cocking his head. He did everything with the pictures but taste them. I was quiet, enjoying the show.

Finally he said, 'Yeah. That's him.'

'You're sure?' I said. 'Would you like more time?'

My humor was lost on him.

'Yeah,' he said. 'I'm sure.'

'He's the man who came to see you and asked that you find someone to intimidate Sarah and then me?'

'Yes,' he said. 'I'm not, of course, saying any of this in court. But it's him.'

He frowned suddenly.

'Hey,' he said. 'You're not wired, are you?'

'Now you ask,' I said. 'But no. I'm not.'

'How do I know?'

'Because I just told you,' I said. 'And you trust me completely.'

'Well, I… oh, fuck,' he said, and took a bite of his cheeseburger.

'Did Mr Franklin say anything about why he wanted you to intimidate us?'

Karp chewed on his cheeseburger a minute and swallowed, and washed it down with a little coffee.

'Just showed me the cash,' he said.

'What better reason?' I said.

He nodded. His cheeseburger was gone.

'If there's nothing else,' he said. 'I gotta run.'

'There's nothing else,' I said.

'You got the check this time?' he said.

'This time,' I said.

'Thanks, nice talking to you,' he said.

He finished his coffee in a long swallow and put the cup down. He stood.

'Thanks for lunch,' he said.

I smiled. He headed for the door. I picked up the uneaten half of my tuna sandwich and took a bite. Crime fighting was hungry business.

36

It was raining hard outside. I was sitting against the wall at the far end of my loft, rolling a tennis ball to the other end. When I rolled it, Rosie would race the length of the loft, snatch it, and trot back to me proudly, give me the ball, turn, and wait quivering with intent for me to throw it again. Rosie disliked the rain and refused to walk in it, so I had to improvise. I'd been doing it for twenty minutes when my phone rang. I rolled the ball down the loft again and went and picked it up.

'Miss Randall?'

'Yes.'

'This is George Markham.'

Rosie was back at my feet, dropping the ball and picking it up and dropping it and picking it up. I bent over and got it and tossed it down the loft again.

'How are you, Mr Markham?'

'I'm terrible, thank you. This stupid investigation has disrupted my home life, badly upset my wife, and estranged me from my daughter.'

'I'm sorry to hear that,' I said.

Rosie brought the ball back and dropped it and picked it up.

'I'm determined to bring it to a conclusion,' George said.

'Excuse me for a moment, Mr Markham.'

I put the phone down and looked Rosie dead in the eyes and said, 'That's it,' and made a safe sign with my spread hands. Rosie stared at me with her impenetrable black eyes. I held the safe sign and stared back at her. We held our positions for a moment. I could hear Rosie breathing around the ball in her mouth. Then she turned and walked off – haughtily, I thought – and jumped on my bed and began to chew the ball.

'Sorry,' I said into the phone. 'What are you planning to do?'

'I'll have the damned DNA test,' he said. 'I find it demeaning and very, very infuriating. But I'm going to do it.'

'That seems sensible,' I said. 'Would you like help arranging it?'

'No. I just want you to know I'm going to do it so we can put the damned issue at rest.'

'Will your wife take one, too?'

'She will not. She is far too angry and upset. She would find it humiliating. And she would find it spiritually compromising.'

'Really?' I said. '"Spiritually compromising."'

'My wife is a spiritual person,' he said.

'And God bless her for it,' I said. 'For this to have the desired effect, it will need to be a reputable lab, not some DNA-R-Us outfit you found on the internet.'

'I'll do it through my local hospital,' Markham said. 'It will be legitimate.'

From the bed, Rosie eyed me while she chewed the ball. I felt like Mommie Dearest.

'I applaud your decision, Mr Markham.'

'Well, I hope once it is done that you will, for God's sake, leave us alone.'

'I'll leave you alone when Sarah is confident of her parentage,' I said.

'Bitch,' George Markham said, and hung up the phone. I hung up on my end, and looked at Rosie, glaring at me from the bed.

'Gee,' I said. 'He thinks so, too.'

37

At 10:30 in the morning, after Rosie and I had run, and I was having a croissant and coffee at my breakfast table, I called Peter Franklin.

'So,' Peter said, 'what happened to you?'

I tried to sound embarrassed.

'I... my ex-husband just got remarried,' I said. 'And it knocked me for a loop.'

'So you couldn't spend the night?'

'I... no, I couldn't. I'm sorry. I guess I'm still a little fragile.'

'Sure,' Peter said. 'Perfectly understandable. I stand ready to help you with that.'

'How kind.'

'I figured it was my fault,' Peter said. 'You know, I wake up and you're gone. I figured Pete, old buddy, you must be losing the magic.'

'That is the most blatant fishing for a compliment I've heard,' I said.

'You think?' Peter said.

'Yes. But I'll give it to you anyway. You have plenty of magic.'

I could hear the amusement in his voice.

'Aw, hell,' he said.

'So,' Peter said. 'Why did you call?'

'I wanted to talk with you,' I said.

'Aha,' he said. 'The magic lives.'

'Perhaps it is just brought out by the right partner.'

'Talk about fishing for a compliment,' Peter said.

'Okay – you are as magical as anybody I ever slept with,' Peter said.

'How nice of you to say so.'

I broke off a piece of croissant and ate it. I could imagine Peter at the other end of the phone. In his office with his feet up. His coat was probably off. He probably wore suspenders. He was so Princetonian, so good-looking, so nice. His eyes had perfect little crinkles at the corners. His hands were well cared for, and strong-looking. His hair perfectly cut. His cologne charming.

'So,' he said. 'That Ike Rosen thing. You ever make any sense of that?'

'No,' I said. 'I'm not sure anyone could make sense of Ike Rosen.'

'The bar association never could,' Peter said.

'Do you do entertainment law exclusively?' I said.

'Mostly,' Peter said.

His voice got the serious sound that men get when they talk about their work.

'Is it fun?'

'More fun probably than criminal law.'

Peter's voice had a smile in it.

'The clientele isn't necessarily nicer,' he said. 'But they're less dangerous.'

'Have you thought about me meeting Lolly Drake?' I said.

'Mostly I've been thinking about why you didn't spend the night.'

'Do I hear a quid pro quo developing?' I said.

'Practicing law includes the art of negotiation,' Peter said.

'Ever the optimist,' I said. 'I know Lolly Drake periodically broadcasts her show from a different city.'

'Sweeps,' Peter said. 'It's a ratings stunt.'

106

'And I know she's coming to Boston,' I said.

'She is,' Peter said. 'Next month.'

'What better time for me to meet her?' I said.

'That might be possible,' he said. 'Under the right circumstances.'

We were both smiling and playful, but we both knew a real negotiation was taking place.

'Of course,' I said, 'under the right circumstances.'

'When?' Peter said.

His voice was light and friendly.

'COD,' I said.

'After you've met Lolly?' he said.

'Yes.'

'That's cold,' he said.

'Not long after,' I said.

He made a sound that might have been a short laugh.

'You don't seem like a drooling fan to me,' Peter said. 'Why are you so hot to meet her?'

If there was a connection between Lolly Drake and Sarah Markham, it was through Peter, and he would know it. He would also know that my interest was professional. Pretending hero worship was silly. Directness was often thought charming.

'Sarah Markham's father worked at the same radio station she did,' I said. 'In Moline, Illinois, in 1981 or so.'

Peter didn't find it charming.

'Jesus Christ,' Peter said. 'You want me to arrange a meeting so you can ask her about a case you're working on?'

'Yes.'

'You're crazy,' he said. 'What the hell has one thing got to do with another?'

'That's what I want to ask her,' I said.

'Listen, Sunny. I like you. We had a good time together one night. But if you think that entitles you to some kind of special discount... I can't arrange any meetings for you with Lolly Drake.'

'The night together was what it was, Peter,' I said. 'But you can't blame a girl for asking.'

107

For a moment the banter went out of Peter Franklin's voice. He said, 'You stay away from Lolly Drake, Sunny.'

'Will you be coming up to Boston when she does her show?' I said.

He was silent for a moment. When he spoke, his voice was careful.

'I could,' he said.

'I'd be happy to see you,' I said.

'I'd like to see you, too,' he said.

We were quiet for a moment. Then Peter spoke again in the cold voice.

'You understand me about Lolly,' he said.

'Sure,' I said. 'Call me when you get to Boston.'

'And you in New York,' he said.

We hung up. Obviously, I couldn't bribe him with sex. Maybe I should be offended. On the other hand, sex probably wasn't that difficult for Peter to come by. And Lolly Drake was.

38

Sarah Markham called and said she wanted to see me. I suggested lunch at Spike's, and when she showed up there at ten after noon, Rosie and I were already in a booth. Spike was behind the bar. He shot his forefinger at Sarah when she came in, and Sarah smiled slightly at him.

'They let you bring your dog?' she said as she sat down.

Rosie wagged her tail and put her face up so Sarah could kiss her if she wished, which, foolishly, she apparently didn't.

'I'm friends with the owner.'

'Spike,' Sarah said.

'Un-huh.'

'What about the Board of Health?'

'Shh,' I said. 'Rosie will hear you.'

Sarah smiled without much energy. Miranda came by. I was having iced tea. Sarah asked for beer.

'I didn't really have any real reason,' she said, 'to ask you to see me.'

'All reasons are real,' I said.

'I feel so isolated. I mean, I'm, like, investigating my parents. Woody is long gone.'

'The boyfriend.'

'Ex-boyfriend. Ever since those two guys beat him up.'

Her beer came. She drank it from the bottle.

'So, you're alone and frightened and lonely,' I said.

'Yes.'

'That's a good reason to come see me,' I said.

'It's weird,' she said. 'The only person I'm okay with is some stranger I hired.'

'We're not strangers now,' I said. 'How is it at home?'

'Awful. My father is, like, hurt, all the time. My mother...' She shook her head. 'Basically, my mother won't speak to me.'

'Who have you been closest to, growing up?' I said.

'My father.'

'Me, too,' I said.

'Was your mother bitchy?' Sarah said.

'She was, ah, difficult.'

'Did she love you?'

'Oh, yes, I think so. But she was limited. She could only love me if I did things that made her feel good.'

'So it was really about her and not you?'

'Maybe a little more complicated,' I said.

'My mother hates me.'

'Straight-out?' I said.

'Yes. She has always hated me.'

'Uncomplicated, I suppose. Why does she hate you?'

'Maybe because I'm not hers.'

'She says you're hers.'

'Not to me,' Sarah said.

'I know,' I said. 'You mentioned that. Do you have any suspicion, no matter how wild or childish, as to whose kid you might be if you aren't theirs?'

'No.'

'Your father has agreed to have the DNA testing.'

'I know. He seems to feel very bad about it.'

'You'll have to supply a sample,' I said.

She nodded.

'Tell me about the trust fund,' I said.

'My mother's father left me some money in a trust fund. When I was eighteen, it came to me.'

'What was your grandfather's name?'

'Carter.'

'That your mother's maiden name?'

'Yes.'

'What was his first name?'

'I don't know. He died before I was born. He's always been just Grandpa Carter.'

'Grandmother?'

'No. None of my grandparents are alive.'

'Aunts and uncles?'

She shook her head.

'So, obviously no cousins,' I said.

'No.'

'And no current boyfriends?'

'Even if I did,' Sarah said. 'I never went out with anybody worth anything.'

'Well, that is pretty much alone,' I said.

'You live alone?' she said.

'I live with Rosie,' I said.

'You know what I mean.'

I nodded.

'Maybe if I were older,' Sarah said. 'Like you. Maybe I wouldn't mind it so much.'

'You might,' I said.

'Do you?'

I thought about how to phrase it.

'I do mind it,' I said. 'And I don't.'

'What the hell does that mean?' Sarah said.

'I'm not sure yet,' I said.

'You just said it, and you don't know what it means?'

'I want someone in my life,' I said. 'But I can't stand to live with anyone.'

'That's weird,' Sarah said.

'Almost certainly,' I said.

'You ever live with anyone?'

'Yes.'

'And it didn't work out?'

'No.'

'You broke up?'

'We got divorced,' I said.

'You were married?'

I looked at her and smiled. 'Duh?' I said.

She thought about it, then smiled and nodded, and said, 'Duh.'

Rosie had given up on the possibility that food would be served and was sprawled on her side next to me, snoring quietly, with my hand resting on her rib cage.

'Was that why you got divorced?' Sarah asked.

'At the time, I thought it was Richie,' I said, 'that he pressed me too hard.'

'For what?' Sarah said.

'For intimacy, for children, for… I don't know. He wanted too much of me.'

'I wish somebody wanted too much of me,' Sarah said.

'I know,' I said. 'When you're alone, you think there couldn't be too much affection. When you get too much, and you don't like it, you think, *What's wrong with me*?'

'Did you think you loved him?' Sarah said.

'I know I did.'

'Do you now?'

'I think so.'

'Do you think you might get back together?'

I shook my head. 'He's remarried,' I said.

'People don't always stay married,' Sarah said.

I smiled. 'I don't think it's in my best interest,' I said, 'to hang around hoping his marriage will fail.'

'This is pretty amazing,' Sarah said.

'That I'm divorced?'

'That you got problems. You're, like, this really together babe.'

'Thank you,' I said.

'You even got a cool dog.'

'I do have a cool dog,' I said.

'You're, like, not scared of things. Like everything's under control. Like you know what to do and you know you'll be able to do it.'

'Sometimes,' I said.

'But not always?'

'I doubt that there is anything that's always.'

'But you're always good at being a detective,' Sarah said.

I saw where this was going. If she couldn't trust me, she had no one at all. And she was right.

'I am excellent at being a detective,' I said.

Miranda came over and put a large platter of nachos on the table between us. Rosie sat up alertly.

'*Amuse-bouche,*' Miranda said. 'From Spike.'

I looked at Sarah and smiled. 'I have cool friends,' I said, 'too.'

39

Brian Kelly called me.

'I'm working homicide,' he said. 'Last year or so. And we got a stiff in Park Square with your business card in his wallet.'

'What's the name?'

'George Markham,' Brian said.

'Suspicious nature?' I said.

'He was shot.'

'You there?' I said.

'Yeah. Parking lot behind the Castle. I thought you might want to stop by.'

'I do,' I said, and hung up the phone.

The Castle, in Park Square, is a gray granite building that was once a National Guard armory and looks like a medieval fortress. They use it now for trade shows and other events. There were half a dozen police cars parked on Huntington Avenue in front of the Castle, and a bunch more in and around the parking lot off Arlington Street. Lights were set up in the parking lot, and the place looked like a movie set. When I pulled up, a uniform stopped me.

'Crime scene, ma'am. Can't park here.'

'Brian Kelly asked me to come down,' I said.

'Sit right there,' the uniform said.

He walked over to a cluster of plainclothes people that included Brian. They were looking down at something. The uniform spoke to Brian, who nodded and half turned and waved me in. I parked next to an EMT vehicle and got out.

'Detective Kelly's over there,' the uniform said.

I smiled and said thank you. I decided not to tell him that I had slept with Detective Kelly and would have recognized him anywhere. What the plainclothes group was looking at was the late George Markham. When I joined them, Brian put his arm around me and gave me a squeeze.

'Frank,' he said to one of the other cops. 'Sunny Randall. Sunny, Frank Belson.'

Belson was very lean, midsized, and clean-shaven, though he showed what must have been an eternal five-o'clock shadow.

'Phil Randall's kid,' he said.

I nodded. We shook hands.

'Liked your old man,' Belson said, and squatted on his heels next to the body.

'What have we got?' I said.

'So far, looks like he took one in the chest, and one in the middle of the forehead.'

'The one in the head to make sure?' I said.

'Reasonable guess,' Belson said. 'There's powder burns around the head wound. Haven't dug out a slug yet but it looks like standard-issue. A nine, or a thirty-eight, maybe.'

Belson stood and began to walk through the crime.

'Vic's walking along here,' Belson said. 'Shooter appears about here, shoots him in the chest. Vic falls over backwards. Shooter walks over, puts the gun against his forehead, and makes sure.'

'Don't sound like a robbery gone bad,' Brian said.

'No,' Belson said. 'It don't.'

He stood, looking at the crime scene, as if he were taking slow-exposure pictures.

'Sunny,' Belson said, 'whyn't you tell Brian what you know about the vic?'

'Sure,' I said.

'And when you see your old man,' Belson said, 'give him my best.'

I said I would, and turned and followed Brian into the Castle, where they had set up temporarily for business.

40

Three days after the funeral, Brian went with me to see Mrs Markham in her silent Andover living room. Sarah wasn't there.

'Is your daughter home, Mrs Markham?' Brian asked.

'No.'

'We'll need to talk with her as well,' Brian said.

'I don't know where she is.'

'Could she be at school?' I said.

'I don't know.'

'Is she okay?' I said.

'I hope not,' Mrs Markham said. 'She killed her father and you helped her.'

'Tell me about that,' Brian said.

'If the two of them hadn't harassed the poor man to death about who was whose parent, he'd be alive today.'

'His death was connected to Sarah's parentage?' Brian said.

'You think it's a coincidence?'

'Who might have killed him?' Brian said.

'I can't imagine,' Mrs Markham said. 'He was a fine man.'

'And Sarah's father?' Brian said.

'Of course.'

'So how is his death connected?' Brian asked.

'I don't think it's a coincidence. They'll probably get me, too.'

'"They"?' Brian said.

'Whoever killed my George.'

'Could you make a guess who that is?' Brian asked.

'How would I know. But if the little bitch hadn't started asking all these questions, her father would be alive.'

'The little bitch being your daughter?' Brian said.

'And her friend here.'

Brian nodded. 'Before his death,' Brian said, 'Mr Markham told people that he was going to get a DNA test to prove he was Sarah's father.'

I was the people Markham told, as far as Brian knew. He was obviously trying to keep me out of it.

'That's nonsense,' Mrs Markham said.

'So he didn't get DNA testing?'

'No, of course not.'

Brian nodded and wrote in his notebook.

'Why wouldn't he,' Brian said, 'or you?'

'If our word isn't sufficient to our own daughter, then we will not further humiliate ourselves and submit to a dehumanizing pseudoscience test.'

Brian nodded and wrote.

'And you haven't any other thoughts on who might have killed your husband?'

Mrs Markham glared at me.

'I don't know who pulled the trigger,' Mrs Markham said. 'But I know who killed him.'

'Do you have a family doctor?' Brian said.

'No. Neither George nor I have ever been sickly.'

'If you had to go to the hospital,' Brian said, 'where would you go?'

'I don't need a hospital,' Mrs Markham said.

'Do you have medical insurance?' Brian said.

'Of course.'

'HMO?'

She nodded. 'Merrimack Health,' she said.

Brian wrote for a little while. Then he put his notebook away and took out his card.

'Anything that you might think of,' he said, 'or anything that happens that might tell us something, please, give me a call. Or, if you prefer, call the Andover police. They'll know how to get me.'

Brian gave her his card. We stood.

'I'm sorry for your loss,' I said to Mrs Markham.

She looked at me in poisonous silence for a moment. 'I don't wish to speak with you,' she said.

In the car, driving, Brian turned and smiled at me.

'Bitch,' he said.

'I see,' I said. 'You believe her.'

'Why wouldn't I?' Brian said. 'She knows you and the kid were responsible because you pushed the question of parentage. But she has no idea who killed him, nor how that connects with you and the kid. Did I miss anything?'

'Not unless I missed it, too,' I said. 'Do you think she got to be fifty years old and has neither a family doctor nor a hospital to which she would go?'

'No.'

'You have the name of her HMO,' I said. 'That was smart.'

'I do, and it was,' Brian said. 'We can see if the Markhams submitted any claims for treatment.'

'The question is,' I said, 'does she know something that she's not sharing, or is she just trying to find an object for her anger?'

'She always been a fruitcake like that?' Brian said.

'When I first met her she was sweet, and subservient, and eager to please,' I said.

'People can be drunk with grief.'

'Except,' I said, 'I didn't see a lot of grief. I saw a lot of rage, but no grief.'

Brian nodded. 'She didn't seem too griefy to me,' he said. 'How about the daughter?'

'I need to find her. If her mother treated her the way she treated me, right after her father's death…'

Brian looked at the dashboard clock.

'You think she's at school?' he said.

'Worth a try,' I said.

'Taft?' he said.

'Yes. You might want to use the siren.'

'You think she's suicidal?' he said.

'I don't know,' I said.

'I'll call the campus police,' Brian said. 'See if they can locate her.'

Brian turned the siren on, and the blue light on the dashboard, and drove faster.

41

The campus police had Sarah in an interview room at the campus police station.

'Why did the cops come?' she said when I came in.

'This is Brian Kelly,' I said. 'He's a Boston police detective.'

'I don't care,' Sarah said. 'Why did the cops come and get me?'

There was a conference table and six chairs, but she was standing with her arms folded tightly across her chest.

'We were worried about you,' I said. 'We wanted to be sure you were all right.'

She stared at me.

'All right?' she said. 'Of course I'm not fucking all right. My father's dead and it's my fault. How fucking all right is that?'

Brian somehow managed to fade from the confrontation a little. He didn't move much, but it was clearly my conversation.

'It is not your fault,' I said. 'It is the fault of the person who shot him.'

'And if I hadn't gotten this crazy bug in my bonnet,' Sarah said, 'he'd still be fine.'

I could almost hear Mrs Markham saying 'bug in your bonnet.'

'Sarah, there is something terribly wrong in your family.'

'Yeah,' Sarah said. 'Me.'

'No,' I said. 'Not you. You're the one who saw it. Your parents don't remember things that everyone remembers. Your father lied about his past. A simple, painless DNA comparison would have answered your concerns. Neither of them would submit.'

'My father was going to,' she said. 'They got the swab from me.'

'Where?'

'I did it at the college infirmary.'

'Do you know if he did it?'

'No.'

'Do you know, if he had, where he'd have done it?'

'No.'

'The infirmary will know where they sent the swab,' Brian said.

I nodded.

'Why do you care now?' Sarah said.

'Maybe it had something to do with his death,' I said.

'You mean someone didn't want him to?'

'I don't know. But he died shortly after he decided to do the DNA test.'

'That's crazy.'

'Yes,' I said. 'It is. And it's crazy that somebody hired men to beat you up. And it's crazy that your mother won't do the DNA comparison. And you're the one that saw the craziness first. You had to do what you did. Someone had to. There was something fundamentally wrong in your family. We still don't know what. But we will.'

'I wish I'd never started all this,' she said.

'I don't blame you. It's a lot nastier than you expected it to be. But I'm with you. And the cops are with you. And we'll hang in there together until we find out why.'

Sarah sat down suddenly at the conference table and folded her arms on the tabletop and put her face down on them.

'I loved him, you know,' she said.

Her voice was muffled.

'Sure, I know,' I said. 'I love my father.'

'Even if he wasn't my father. I loved him. Mostly, he was nice to me.'

'Regardless of biology,' I said. 'He was your father.'

She nodded her buried head without speaking.

'I need to ask you one more question,' I said.

Sarah nodded, her face still down.

'How do you get your trust money?' I said.

'It just shows up in my checking account every month,' she said.

'Wire transfer?'

'I guess so.'

'From where?'

'I don't know.'

'Where do you have your checking account?' I said.

'Pequot Bank.'

'Here in Walford?'

'Yes. On Oak Street, right across from the student union.'

'And before you came to Taft?'

'I didn't get it,' Sarah said. 'I wasn't old enough.'

'When does it come?'

'First of the month.'

I looked at Brian. He nodded and tapped himself on the chest.

'Okay,' I said.

She stayed the way she was. I looked at Brian. He shook his head slightly and shrugged and turned his palms up.

'Are you rooming with anyone?'

She shook her head.

'Boyfriend?'

Shake.

'Would you like to go home?'

'No.'

I didn't blame her.

I looked at Brian. He looked at me. He smiled faintly. I nodded slowly and took a deep breath and let it out.

'I want you to come stay with Rosie and me for a while,' I said.

Sarah was silent. Her face was still down on the table, resting on her forearms. She didn't move.

Then, without looking up, she said, 'Okay.'

I looked at Brian again. He was staring up at the ceiling.

'While we're packing,' I said to him, 'maybe you could check where the infirmary sent the DNA sample?'

'Let's have Sarah join us,' Brian said. 'They'll be more cooperative if the donor is doing the asking.'

'Okay with you, kiddo?'

She was sitting up now, looking at us.

'I guess so,' she said. 'What about the school? If I don't go to class, I'll get in trouble.'

'I'll talk to the school,' Brian said. 'If the dean is a woman, I'll charm her. If it's a man, I'll frighten him.'

Sarah almost smiled. 'It's a woman,' she said.

'Oh, good,' Brian said. 'Charming is so much easier than scary.'

'It is?' I said. 'I can't usually tell which you're being.'

Sarah actually did smile, though very slightly.

42

Life Form Laboratory was in the rear of the second floor of an old brick building on Albany Street near Boston Medical Center. The director talked with Sarah and me in her tiny office overlooking a narrow parking lot.

'I don't know if I can release this information,' the director said.

She was a lanky, gray-haired woman, wearing rimless glasses.

'Sarah is one of the two donors,' I said.

'But the actual testing was requested by the other donor.'

'Who is now a murder victim,' I said.

The director frowned. She looked like everyone's stereotype

of an elementary-school principal. And she clearly disapproved of people being murdered.

'Oh,' she said to Sarah, 'how dreadful. Were you related?'

'He was my father,' Sarah said.

'The biological relationship may be an important part of the murder investigation,' I said. 'We can do this informally, or we can come back with the police and a court order. And the cops will probably close you down while they search all the records, and the press will probably learn of it and your name will be in the paper as part of a murder investigation.'

'Are you threatening me, Ms Randall?'

'I prefer to think of it as warning you,' I said.

She looked at me sternly. I smiled my sweet, young, blonde-girl smile. She nodded as if she was confirming something with herself.

'Well, surely,' the director said, 'since this young woman is one of the donors, I don't see a problem.'

'Thank you,' Sarah said.

The director stood, turned to her computer, and tapped the keyboard for a moment and sat back. We waited. She studied the screen.

'I'll print this out for you,' she said, and tapped the keyboard again. 'But I can tell you that it is not a match.'

I heard Sarah breathe in.

'He's not my father?'

'You do not share his DNA.'

The printer on the top of a file cabinet began to hum, and in a moment the printout came sliding forth and the printer went silent. No one spoke for a moment.

'You're sure?' Sarah said.

'Yes.'

'You couldn't have made a mistake?'

'Very unlikely.'

Sarah looked at me. She was breathing quickly, as if she was a little short of breath.

'Now you know,' I said.

She nodded and didn't say anything.

'When did Mr Markham get the results?' I said to the director.

She looked at her computer screen.

'Five days ago,' she said.

'Two days before he died,' I said.

'Who the hell is my father?' Sarah said.

I was startled. I had begun to think of this as a murder case. But for Sarah it was still paternity-related.

'Before we're through,' I said, 'you and I will find out.'

'And is she my mother?'

'I don't know,' I said.

The director looked uncomfortable. This was very unscientific.

'I'll bet she isn't,' Sarah said.

'You're sure he received this information?' I said to the director.

She looked at her screen some more.

'Yes, we overnighted it to him, and he signed for it.'

I took the printout and folded it and slipped it into my bag. I looked at Sarah. She was still short of breath. Her face was pale, with reddish smudges on her cheekbones. She looked like she had a fever.

'Anything else you wish to ask the director?' I said to her.

She shook her head. I nodded and stood and put my hand out to the director.

'Thanks for your help,' I said.

She stood and shook my hand.

'I hope things work out,' she said, not at all sternly.

Then she looked at Sarah. 'DNA is not the only thing that makes a parent,' she said, and put her hand gently on Sarah's shoulder.

Sarah nodded and stood. I put a hand on her arm and steered her out of the office and down the narrow back stairwell to where we'd parked on the street. In the car, we were quiet. I started up and drove slowly toward Mass Avenue. Sarah rode with her head turned away from me, looking out the window.

Without looking at me, she said, 'If he's not my father, and she's not my mother... who the fuck am I?'

We stopped for the light at Mass Avenue. I had nothing to say. I put my right hand out and patted her thigh. Then the light changed and I turned left toward the expressway.

43

I settled into my chair next to her desk. The box of Kleenex was there, where it always was. She was at her desk, sitting sideways, facing me, her chair slightly tilted, her legs crossed. Today she had on a camel-colored suit with a wine-colored top, and a quiet gold necklace.

'I was thinking about my Rosie dream,' I said.

Dr Silverman nodded.

'Do you understand about dogs?' I said.

'Yes.'

'Do you have a dog?'

'Yes.'

My God, two personal revelations. She must really like me.

'Then you know,' I said, 'the degree to which one can love them.'

She nodded her head once, very slightly. Getting herself back under control.

'I realize this isn't a breakthrough discovery, but I think the dream was symbolic.'

Dr Silverman looked noncommittal.

'And I think, in the dream, Rosie is love.'

Dr Silverman cocked her head slightly and raised her eyebrows. It was her code for 'Please pursue the thought.'

'If she represents love, and in the dream, I'm afraid because she's off her leash...'

She nodded her head very slightly, so that it was barely visible, another clue that said 'Keep going.' Sometime, I'd have to ask why tiny clues were okay, but you weren't allowed to say, 'Oh, boy, that's interesting!'

'Help me with this,' I said. 'Are dreams warnings? Wish fulfillments? What?'

'Dreams are sometimes simply dramatizations of the circumstance we are in.'

'It's saying this is how you are?'

'Maybe.'

'It's not saying this is how you want to be?'

'Probably not,' she said.

'Okay, so I'm afraid to what? Let my love off the leash?'

'You say in the dream Rosie running loose makes you fearful?'

'Yes.'

'Of what?'

'I'll lose her.'

'Lose love?' Dr Silverman said.

'Yeah, I guess so.'

'In dreams, things often represent more than one thing.'

I sat. Dr Silverman waited.

'Me?' I said.

She smiled. *Bingo! What a good girl am I.*

'But not instead of love. Rosie is love, and Rosie is me, and I'm afraid I'll lose love if I let go, and I'm afraid I'll lose what? Me, if I let it run?'

I was excited. I felt like something was happening.

'And you felt how when you thought of the dream afterwards?'

'While I was awake?'

Nod.

'I liked it that Rosie was running free,' I said. 'The opposite of how I felt in the dream.'

Dr Silverman nodded.

'So, which is it?' I said.

'Both,' Dr Silverman said.

44

I came home from Dr Silverman's with my head resonating inarticulately. Sarah was watching television at the far end of the loft, smoking cigarettes and drinking Coke. Someday, I'd have to discuss smoking in my home, but today was not the time. There was a message on my answering machine to call Detective Second-Grade Eugene Corsetti, Manhattan homicide. I sat on my bed and hugged Rosie until she rebelled, then I called Detective Corsetti.

'Thanks for calling back,' he said. 'Just routine. I got a homicide down here, and the vic had your business card in his wallet.'

'Who's the victim?' I said.

A part of me already knew what Corsetti would say.

'Lawyer, fella named Peter Franklin.'

'I know him,' I said.

'Can you tell me what your relationship was?'

'How did he die?' I said.

'Your relationship to the victim?'

'If you have my card, you know I'm a private detective,' I said.

'I do,' Corsetti said.

'He was connected sort of indirectly to a case I'm working on.'

'How so?' Corsetti said.

I thought how to phrase it.

'Oh, God,' I said. 'I'll come down there.'

'We can probably do this by phone,' Corsetti said.

'No, it's complicated. And maybe you can help me, too.'

'For the record,' Corsetti said. 'Were you in New York last night, between about six p.m. and midnight?'

'I was here,' I said. 'Having dinner with a young woman and a male friend at the male friend's restaurant.'

'Could I get phone numbers?'

'The young woman is here,' I said. 'I'll put her on. The man's

125

name is Spike, and I'll give you the restaurant phone number.'

'What's Spike's last name?'

I told him and then I put Sarah on and she confirmed.

Back on the phone, I said to Corsetti, 'How did he die?'

'I'll check with the restaurant, but you sound okay to me.'

'Damn it,' I said. 'How did he die?'

'He was executed,' Corsetti said. 'Shot once in the chest that put him down, and once in the head. Perp pressed the muzzle right against his forehead.'

'I'll drive down in the morning. Can I see you, say, at one?'

'Sure,' he said. 'You don't have to come to the station. I'll meet you someplace.'

'Saint Regis Hotel?' I said. 'In the lobby?'

Corsetti whistled softly.

'Pretty snazzy for a shoofly,' Corsetti said.

'I'm a pretty snazzy shoofly,' I said.

'Besides looking for someone snazzy,' Corsetti said, 'how do I recognize you?'

'Five-seven, one hundred thirty pounds, blond hair, late thirties.'

'What'll you be wearing?' Corsetti said.

'Tomorrow?' I said. 'How do I know what I'll be wearing tomorrow?'

'Dumb question,' Corsetti said, and hung up.

45

Detective Corsetti and I sat in a couple of wine-and-gold armchairs in the lobby of the St. Regis, to the right of the front desk, and talked about the murder of Peter Franklin. Corsetti wasn't very tall, only about my height. But laterally, he filled the armchair entirely, and very little of his width appeared to be fat.

'You're right,' Corsetti said. 'You are snazzy.'

'You're kind of cute yourself,' I said.

'I know,' Corsetti said. 'Talk to me about Franklin.'

'I was hired,' I said, 'by a young woman who doubts that her parents are really hers. One day, two thugs beat her up and told her to lay off. I tracked them back to Franklin. They say he hired them.'

'You talk to him?' Corsetti said.

He was more casually dressed than some of the St. Regis patrons. He had on a leather bomber jacket, and an adjustable Yankee's cap worn backwards.

'Yes.'

'Lemme guess,' Corsetti said. 'He denied everything.'

'Almost. One link in the connection was a disbarred lawyer named Ike Rosen.'

Corsetti made a note of the name.

'In New York, or Boston?' Corsetti said.

'New York, West Ninety-second Street.'

Corsetti wrote that down.

'What was the connection?'

'Rosen worked for the same firm as Franklin, until they fired him.'

Corsetti scribbled again.

'You coulda told me this on the phone,' he said. 'What else you got?'

'The young woman that hired me is named Sarah. Her father's name was George...'

'"Was"?'

'I'm getting to that,' I said. 'George used to be a radio announcer. About 1981 or '2, he was working at a radio station in Moline, Illinois. Lolly Drake worked there at the same time, when she was just starting out.'

'Franklin represents her, or did,' Corsetti said.

'You've been busy,' I said.

'Hard to believe I'm still second-grade, isn't it?'

'My guess would be that you might annoy your superiors,' I said.

'Naw, I say it's a height issue,' Corsetti said. 'You said something about George.'

'He finally agreed to a DNA test,' I said. 'And two days later he was shot to death.'

'What about the test?' Corsetti said.

'He is not the girl's biological father,' I said.

Corsetti wrote that in his notebook and then sat back in the tight armchair and tapped his lower teeth with the butt end of his Bic pen.

'How was he shot?' Corsetti said after a time.

'In the chest,' I said. 'Which put him down, and in the forehead, very close.'

'Like Franklin,' Corsetti said.

'Yes.'

'Where?' Corsetti said.

'In a parking lot, back of a building in Boston.'

'Any sign he knew the killer?'

'No.'

'Who's running the case in Boston?'

'Detective sergeant named Frank Belson,' I said.

Corsetti wrote that down in his notebook and looked at his notes for a moment and closed the notebook.

'Franklin lived uptown, on Fifth, opposite the park.'

'Corner of Seventy-sixth,' I said.

Corsetti nodded.

'Doorman said he always ran in the park at night, after work,' Corsetti told me. 'Which was sometimes pretty late, because a lot of times he worked pretty late.'

'That where you found him?'

'Dog walker found him about seven in the morning by the pond, near Seventy-second Street.'

'Shot in the chest,' I said, 'and then in the forehead.'

'Yep.'

'Head shot was from very close.'

'Yep.'

'Any hint he knew the shooter?' I said.

'Nope.'

We were quiet. The lobby was high-ceiling and Gilded Age. Everything gleamed. Some of the people coming and going looked like business travelers. Some looked like tourists. None of them was wearing a baseball cap backward.

'What do you think?' I said.

'You got any ballistics on the gun in Boston?' Corsetti said.

'No.'

'I'll call Belson,' Corsetti said. 'We got a nine-millimeter down here.'

'At the scene, Belson said it could have been a nine.'

'Well,' Corsetti said. 'I don't know what the hell is going on. But we can't assume it's a bunch of coincidences and forget it.'

'No.'

'Where's Lolly Drake fit in?' Corsetti said.

'She knew both victims,' I said.

'So do you,' Corsetti said.

'I got an alibi,' I said.

'I know,' Corsetti said, 'I called that restaurant.'

I smiled. 'I wonder if Lolly's got one.'

'We could ask her,' Corsetti said.

'Ask her?'

'Yeah, she tapes over here on the West Side every afternoon.'

'You want to ask Lolly Drake if she has an alibi for two murders?'

'Sure.'

'Don't you want to clear that with somebody at work?'

Corsetti shook his head.

'I've been a cop,' I said. 'Somebody with a profile like Lolly Drake… you cover yourself.'

Corsetti grinned at me.

'Perhaps you have mistaken me,' he said, 'for someone who gives a shit.'

46

Lolly Drake broadcast from an old theater, way west of Broadway, near the river. There were larger-than-life pictures of

Lolly everywhere in the building. Lolly with movie stars. Lolly with senators. Lolly in Los Angeles. Lolly in Rome. Lolly with a cute dog. Lolly with a foreign dignitary. Lolly in London. Lolly on a horse. Lolly at the White House. Lolly in San Francisco. Lolly on a riverboat. In every picture, her face was framed by thick, auburn hair. Her famous green eyes stared from the photos as if they could penetrate your soul.

While Lolly finished taping her third show of the day, we sat in her office with her manager, whose name was Harvey Delk, and a lawyer named Curtin, from Harrop and Moriarty.

'Lolly will be really drained,' her manager said. 'It's always hard for her to come down on the three-show days.'

Corsetti smiled and nodded pleasantly. He sat in his chair, looking contented, his fingers locked across his stomach. It was a stomach you'd expect to be fat, but it wasn't. Corsetti was built like a bowling ball, and was probably no softer.

It was a big office, and nicely furnished, but utilitarian at heart, with cinder-block walls painted yellow, and a thick, coffee-colored rug over the vinyl flooring. On the monitor, Lolly could be seen sitting on a couch behind a coffee table. When the guest was particularly captivating, she leaned over the coffee table toward him. It allowed a dignified show of cleavage.

'Truth is not merely fact,' she was saying, 'it is also feeling, honestly expressed, don't you think?'

The guest, a young actor promoting a new movie, nodded.

'It's love,' he said, 'and honest passion.'

I looked at Corsetti. He smiled at me benevolently.

On screen, Lolly looked at the audience.

'You know my mantra,' she said. 'Where secrets exist, love cannot.'

The audience applauded. Corsetti nodded vigorously in agreement.

'She's really something,' Corsetti said, 'isn't she?'

'Something,' I said.

'It's what attracted me to the role,' the actor said, 'the authentic honesty of the part.'

'You can be proud of that,' Lolly said. 'Men are beginning to get it.'

'Well, if we are,' the young actor said, 'it's because you ladies have shown us the value of honest emotion.'

Lolly beamed at him.

'And we're getting damned tired of it,' she said.

The audience applauded loudly. Lolly reached across and patted the young actor's hand.

'And the name of the movie again?' she said.

'*Timeless*.'

'And it's opening when?' Lolly said.

'January sixth,' the actor said, 'in New York and LA. January thirteenth in general release.'

Lolly turned her head toward the studio audience. 'I've seen a private screening of *Timeless*,' she said. 'And it's fabulous.'

She looked back at the young actor. 'And you're fabulous in it, Bob.'

She looked into the camera.

'I hope every one of you will see it. Bring the kids. It will do them some good to encounter honest emotion. There's not enough of it around.'

The young actor looked modest. The audience roared into sustained applause. The credits began to roll. Lolly and the young actor began to chat without sound until the screen went gray.

'She really nailed it,' Corsetti said to her manager. 'Not enough honest emotion these days. Is that right on the money, or what?'

The manager was a heavy young man, wearing an oversized double-breasted black suit, a white shirt, and a platinum-colored tie. The suit was probably supposed to conceal his weight. It didn't. Nothing does.

'Miss Drake has a real grasp on the core values of this country,' the manager said.

The door opened and Lolly Drake came in. She was a little older than she looked on camera, but she was good-looking, and her eyes were everything they seemed to be in her pictures.

Her dark green suit was beautifully cut. I paid close attention. My mother had watched Lolly Drake since she had gone national, and worshipped her. It could earn me many points that I'd met her. Lolly stopped inside her office door and looked at us.

'Who are they?' she said to her manager.

'Police, Lolly. You remember, I…'

Lolly nodded impatiently. 'Yes, yes. What do you want?'

Corsetti smiled at her and took out his badge. 'Detective Eugene Corsetti, Miss Drake.'

He nodded at me.

'Sunny Randall,' he said.

'I suppose it's about Peter,' she said.

'It is,' Corsetti said.

'God,' Lolly said, 'just what I need after three shows.'

'It's a great pleasure to meet you, ma'am,' Corsetti said.

'Yeah, sure,' Lolly said. 'Let's get this over with.'

She went to her big semicircular desk and sat behind it.

'I'll give you ten minutes,' she said.

'Oh, I'm sure that'll be plenty, Miss Drake,' Corsetti said.

'How about your partner?' Lolly said. 'Does she talk?'

'When I have something to say,' I said.

'Is that a remark?' Lolly said.

'No, ma'am,' I said. 'Just the honest expression of my circumstance.'

Lolly frowned. 'Don't get chippy with me, girlie.'

'Okay,' I said.

'Your ten minutes are ticking,' Lolly said to Corsetti.

'Yes, ma'am,' Corsetti said. 'Of course you knew Peter Franklin.'

'Of course.'

'And George Markham.'

'Who?'

'George Markham, ma'am,' Corsetti said.

'I never heard of him.'

'You and he worked together at a radio station in Moline in the early 1980s,' Corsetti said.

Lolly glanced at her manager. Her manager glanced at the lawyer. The lawyer frowned at Corsetti.

'What on earth are you talking about?' Lolly said after a time.

Corsetti looked at me.

'Sunny?' he said.

'You had a call-in radio show at WMOL Moline called *Lolly's Law*. During that same time period, George Markham was an announcer at the station.'

'And I'm supposed to remember every loser I worked with at some five-thousand-watt station in East Bumfuck?' Lolly said.

'Never forgot where she came from,' Corsetti said to me.

I smiled. Lolly looked a little startled. What happened to her drooling fan?

'Anything else?' Lolly said.

'You have any idea why somebody would want to kill Markham?'

'Kill him? I told you, I don't even remember him.'

'Peter Franklin was your lawyer,' Corsetti said.

'I already said he was.'

Corsetti nodded happily.

'Do you know why he hired some people to beat up George Markham's daughter?'

Lolly stared at Corsetti. She opened her mouth and closed it without speaking. She looked at her manager and at her lawyer. Then she seemed to rally.

'You dreadful little man,' she said.

'I'm not little,' Corsetti said. 'Just short.'

'I don't care what you are,' Lolly said. 'I am through wasting my time with you.'

'This interview is terminated,' the lawyer said, 'as of now.'

'Interview?' Corsetti said. 'You think this is a fucking interview? I'm questioning a suspect in a double homicide, and the questioning stops when I say it stops.'

'Perhaps you should tell us what this is all about,' the lawyer said.

He was an entertainment lawyer. A good criminal lawyer would have terminated the discussion right there. Corsetti didn't have enough to arrest her. But Corsetti got some credit for that. He had concealed the limits of what he knew, and implied that it was more than it was. So the lawyer still didn't know what we had.

'George Markham's daughter, Sarah, hired Sunny Randall to establish her paternity. Peter Franklin hired some guys to make Sarah stop. And then to try to make Sunny Randall stop. Then George Markham got shot, and a couple days later, Peter Franklin got shot, in the same manner that Markham did, a shot in the chest that knocked him down. A bullet in the forehead, point-blank, to be sure they were dead. Miss Drake knew Markham, and she knew Franklin.'

'Hired this woman?' Lolly said.

Corsetti nodded.

'You told us she was a police officer.'

'No,' Corsetti said, 'I told you I was a police officer. I told you she was Sunny Randall. Which she is.'

'You implied.'

Corsetti grinned and shook his head. 'You inferred,' he said.

'I'll have your badge,' Lolly said.

The lawyer made a placating gesture with his hand.

'Lolly,' he said.

'Don't you Lolly me, you fucking wimp,' she said. 'I want his badge.'

'Can't have it,' Corsetti said. 'Captain says I'm supposed to have one.'

'Get out,' Lolly said.

'Do you have anything you'd like to share with me about these murders, Miss Drake?' Corsetti said.

'Miss Drake,' the lawyer said.

'Shut up,' she said.

She stood and walked around her desk and leaned toward Corsetti.

'You came in here and pretended this floozy was a police detective. You imply that I am guilty of some preposterous crime. I will see to it, with every power I have at my command, that you are sorry. Do you actually think you can stand up to me? Do you have any idea who and what I am?'

'A highfalutin asshole,' Corsetti said. 'Am I right or wrong?'

Lolly jerked back as if he'd struck her. Her face reddened as if she might cry. Then she turned and ran out of the office. Corsetti stood as she left and jerked his head at me.

'Have a nice day,' he said to the two men, and we went out.

Riding down in the elevator, Corsetti looked at me and grinned.

'Floozy?' he said.

'How did she know?' I said.

47

I met my father for lunch at a coffee shop on Summer Street on my side of the Fort Point Channel. He always looked the same to me. He probably wasn't. He was more than thirty years older than he was when he took me to nursery school for the first time. He had always been a hands-on father; he'd had to be, given my mother's limitations. It always made me smile when I thought of it. On my first day at school, I hadn't cried. And he had.

'You know this business well enough,' my father said, 'to know that coincidences exist.'

'But assuming that they are coincidences doesn't get you anywhere,' I said.

'And assuming they aren't gets you where you don't want to be,' my father said.

'So what do I do with Lolly Drake?' I said.

'You could leave it to the New York cops,' my father said.

'You think they can get to her?'

'Not with what they've got so far.'

'No,' I said. 'She's got layers of protection.'

'And not everybody in the chain of command will have the same attitude as your friend Corsetti,' my father said.

'She was so arrogant,' I said. 'I'd love to level her out a little.'

My father's thick hands rested on the tabletop. He turned his coffee cup slowly.

'Not a good idea to make it personal,' he said.

'I'm not a cop, Daddy. I work for me.'

He grinned at me.

'So it's all personal?' he said.

I nodded.

'You don't care about a case,' my father said, 'you don't do it.'

'It's why I left the police,' I said.

'Alternative would be to care about them all.'

'Did you?' I said.

'I tried to.'

'But?'

'But some I didn't give a rat's ass about,' my father said.

'But you did the cases.'

'Yes.'

'And you didn't quit.'

'I had a wife and two daughters,' my father said.

'So you couldn't quit.'

'Have to take care of your family,' my father said.

He smiled at me. 'And generally, I liked the work.'

'And you were good at it,' I said.

'Yeah,' he said. 'I was.'

The waitress brought a fried-egg sandwich for my father, tuna salad for me.

'I don't know where to go with this,' I said.

'You think Markham thought the DNA would prove his paternity?' my father said.

'Why would he take it if it wouldn't?'

'So why would he think it would?' my father said.

'Because he thought he really was her father.'

'And why would a man think someone was his child?'

'Because the child's mother told him,' I said.

The waitress came and refilled our coffee cups, and moved on to fill other cups at other tables.

'So why didn't he take it the moment the question came up?' my father said.

'My best guess,' I said, 'is that Mrs Markham was opposed.'

'And she still won't do it,' my father said.

'DNA? No.'

'So who's the kid's mother?'

'You think she refuses because she knows she's not the mother?' I said.

'Yes.'

'So why conceal it?' I said. 'Lots of people adopt children.'

'But Markham thought the kid – what's her name?'

'Sarah,' I said.

'Markham thought Sarah was his.'

'And Mrs Markham knew she was not hers,' I said.

'So who was Sarah's mother, and why did Markham think he was her father?'

'And why did she... hell, does she... pretend that Sarah is theirs?' I said.

My father dabbed a trace of egg yolk off the corner of his mouth with a paper napkin.

'Tell me about the trust fund,' my father said.

'Money comes from a bank in New York,' I said. 'First of every month. Brian Kelly is on it.'

'Might be interesting to see if any other money comes to that family,' he said.

'Lolly Drake is in on this thing,' I said.

'Maybe she's the momma.'

'Oh, Phil, you said it. I was hoping you would.'

He smiled at me.

'Phil?' he said.

'We're pals, too,' I said.

'Good.'

'You really think she could be the mother?'

'She knew Markham at the right time.'

'I would dearly love to get a DNA sample from her.'

'Not likely,' my father said.

'I can try to establish sexual contact between them, at the appropriate time.'

'Twentysomething years later?'

'Hard, but not impossible.'

'She would have the money to pay somebody off,' my father said.

'And a reason to want to conceal her pregnancy,' I said. 'She bills herself as the voice of the moral majority.'

My father smiled again.

'A phrase from my youth,' he said. 'Or she may just be a coincidence.'

'The hell she is,' I said.

'Either way,' my father said, 'there's two other things I'd be doing. I'd follow the money.'

'I've heard that works,' I said.

My father nodded.

'You can always trust money,' he said.

'What else?' I said.

'Well,' my father said. 'If there's hard evidence, forensic stuff, cops will get it. Or they won't. Either way, you don't do that kind of detecting.'

'I'm not equipped,' I said.

'No, you're not. What you're equipped to do is talk to suspects and witnesses. Which, by the way, you do very well.'

I felt a small thrill of pleasure. My father had complimented me.

'So what you got,' my father said, 'is you got the daughter, who has probably given you most of what she's got. You got Lolly Drake, who is nearly bulletproof. And you've got Mrs Markham.'

'She's probably not told me all she knows,' I said.

'Probably not,' my father said.

'And I can get to her.'

My father nodded.

'We are driving toward a logical assumption here,' I said.

'Was my case,' he said, 'I'd squeeze the hell out of Mrs Markham.'

48

My father and I finished our sandwiches. We were quiet for a moment while we drank our coffee. The waitress asked about dessert.

'I'll have a piece of that pie,' my father said.

The waitress looked at the pie on the counter under the glass dome.

'Oh, let me check what kind,' she said.

'I don't care what kind,' my father said. 'I'll have a slice, with some cheese and more coffee.'

'Certainly.'

The waitress looked at me. I smiled and shook my head. She went to get my father his pie.

'No decaf?' I said.

'I hate decaf,' my father said.

'Most people say as they get older, real coffee keeps them awake.'

'It does.'

'It keeps you awake, but you drink it anyway.'

'I do.'

'You could learn to like decaf,' I said.

'Fuck decaf,' my father said.

'Oh,' I said, 'of course. I hadn't thought of that.'

The waitress came with the pie and cheese. The pie was apple. My father ate it the way he did everything: straight ahead. Without flourish.

'I'm seeing a psychiatrist,' I said.

My father swallowed a mouthful of pie.

'How come?' he said.

'Richie,' I said.

My father nodded.

'Yeah,' he said. 'That's a hard one.'

'One of the things I'm trying to figure out is why it's so hard.'

My father drank some coffee.

'Who's the shrink?' he said.

'Dr Silverman,' I said. 'In Cambridge.'

My father smiled.

'Susan Silverman?' he said.

'Yes, you know her?'

'I do,' he said.

'Tell me about her.'

'No.'

'No?'

'I don't know a ton about shrinkage,' my father said. 'But I'm pretty sure it's not improved by having people talk about your shrink.'

'But you like her?' I said.

'Yes.'

'If you didn't, you'd say so, wouldn't you?'

'I like her,' my father said. 'So I don't have to think about what to say if I didn't.'

I felt slightly chastised.

'Sure,' I said.

'She's a smart woman,' my father said. 'And you're a smart woman. And she's tough. And you're tough. I'm pretty sure you'll do some good things together.'

'We are talking about you and Mother,' I said. I felt like I was confessing.

'I bet most people in therapy, especially early in therapy, are talking about their mother and father,' he said.

'I'm dying to find out how you know Dr Silverman,' I said.

'Ask her,' my father said.

'God,' I said, 'you're as bad as she is.'

'Or as good,' he said.

We looked at each other happily.

'Will you tell Mother?' I said.

'I think I won't.'

'Because?'

'Because it's not information she can make much use of,' my father said.

'Gee, I thought you might give me a speech,' I said, 'about

husbands and wives sharing everything.'

'When's the last time I gave you a speech?' my father said.

'The time in high school when I stayed out all night after a dance.'

'That showed great restraint,' my father said. 'I wanted to kill you.'

The waitress came by and poured us more coffee, and dropped off the check. My father picked it up automatically. I let him, automatically.

'Why do you think Mom wouldn't do well with this?' I said.

My father's pie was gone. I could see him thinking about another piece.

'I love Em,' he said. 'I have loved her for more than forty years. But it doesn't mean I don't see her clearly. She's quick to judge, she's opinionated, and the opinions were formed when she was in her teens.'

'Often wrong but never uncertain,' I said.

He smiled.

'Exactly,' he said.

He looked around for the waitress, caught her eye, and pointed toward his pie plate. She came over.

'Another slice of pie, sir?'

'Yes, please,' my father said.

'It is good,' the waitress said, 'isn't it?'

'It is,' my father said. 'No cheese this time.'

She brought him another slice.

'You know this about her?' I said.

'I've always known her,' he said.

'But you couldn't change her?'

'No,' he said. 'I love her as she is. I always tried to protect you and Elizabeth from the worst of it. I had more success with you than with Elizabeth.'

'Why?'

'You're more like me,' he said. 'But there was no changing Em, and I knew it.'

'Love me or leave me?'

'Yes.'

'And you love her?'

'I do,' my father said.

'And you're happy?'

'Yes,' he said. 'I am.'

He ate some of his pie and drank some of his coffee. I thought of all the suppers and breakfasts I'd seen him eat. I wanted to get up and sit in his lap. I felt a little frightened.

'Elizabeth's kind of a mess, Daddy,' I said.

'I know.'

'And I seem to be kind of messy these days, too.'

'You'll get better,' he said.

'I guess you couldn't protect us from Mother sufficiently.'

'Probably not,' my father said. 'Probably wasn't everything I should have been, either.'

'You were a good father,' I said. 'You never disapproved of me.'

'Not much to disapprove of,' he said, and smiled slightly. 'Except that all-night in high school.'

I felt like crying. When I spoke, my voice was shaky.

'I love you, Daddy.'

'I love you, too,' he said.

'You did what you could.'

'So did your mother,' my father said.

'It wasn't quite enough,' I said.

My father looked straight at me for a moment. I felt fourteen again.

'I think, probably,' he said, 'it never is.'

49

Brian Kelly stopped by for coffee. We had some with the oatmeal-maple scones that he brought, at the counter in my kitchen area. Sarah joined us. As did Rosie. Sarah sat on a stool. Rosie settled in on the floor under my feet and fixed us with her relentless stare.

'Money is wired to Sarah's account,' Brian said. 'From the Wellington Bank in Gillette, Wyoming.'

I said, 'Wyoming?'

'Yep.'

'Where's Gillette, Wyoming?' Sarah said.

'West,' Brian said. 'Money comes from an account belonging to Bright Flower Charitable Foundation.'

'It's from my grandfather,' Sarah said.

Brian shrugged. 'Bright Flower is a P.O. box in New York City,' he said. 'Authorizing signature is "July Fishbein."'

'July?' I said. 'Like the month?'

'Yep, June, July,' Brian said.

'The money comes from my grandfather,' Sarah said.

Brian nodded. He looked down at Rosie.

'This dog want something?' he said.

'Everything,' I said.

'You know anybody named July Fishbein?' he said to Sarah.

'No.'

He looked at me.

'Name means nothing to me,' I said.

'New York DOS says that Bright Flower is a legally incorporated not-for-profit.'

'What's DOS?' Sarah said.

I wanted her to go out and play.

'Department of State,' I said. 'So they have a board.'

'Yep. July Fishbein and four other women.'

'And?'

'New York cops are working on it, but so far we haven't located any of them.'

'Including July?'

Sarah broke off a piece of her scone and gave it to Rosie. Rosie ate it carefully and resumed her stare.

'Is there a phone number?' I said. 'For July or Bright Flower?'

'You bet.'

'Is it real?'

'Nope.'

'What happens when you dial it?'

'Operator interrupt: Number is not in service.'

'What is all this stuff about?' Sarah said. 'What's it mean?'

'Someone is going to considerable length to send you money without anyone knowing who they are,' I said.

'You don't think it's my grandfather?'

'No,' I said.

'Well, who the hell?'

'Maybe your biological father,' Brian said.

'Or mother,' I said.

'You don't think she's my mother, either?' Sarah said.

'She wouldn't do the DNA test,' I said.

'She says she feels it's an insulting intrusion,' Sarah said.

She might not like Mrs Markham, but she liked even less the thought that she was parentless. I didn't blame her.

'You got any other basis for doubting Mrs Markham?' Brian said.

'Not really,' I said.

'But…'

'But I sure as hell would like to know where Lolly Drake fits in.'

'If she fits in,' Brain said.

'She's in here somewhere,' I said. 'She keeps popping up.'

'You think she might be my mother?' Sarah said.

'She keeps popping up,' I said.

We were quiet with our coffee. The scones were gone. Rosie refused to accept the fact, however, and kept up her beady vigil under our feet. Sarah's eyes were teary. She wasn't quite crying, but her voice shook a little.

'Why did I do this?' she said.

'You had a right to know,' I said.

'Why didn't I let it go, and just live as I had? Mother, father, go to college, get a boyfriend, get married. Why didn't I do that. None of this would have happened.'

'You don't know what would have happened,' I said.

She looked at me. Brian was quiet, drinking his coffee. One of his assets as a detective was how still he could be.

'Why did I do this?' she said.

I realized it was not a rhetorical question. She wanted me to tell her.

'You seemed kind of mad at them,' I said.

'You think I did this because I was mad at them?'

'We do a lot of things,' I said, 'for reasons we don't understand. Maybe this was a way to get back at them for not being the parents you wanted.'

A couple months of therapy, and I was Dr Phil.

'So now,' Sarah said, 'if you're right, I got none.'

'Or others,' I said.

'Yeah, right, others. What am I going to do, sleep on your couch the rest of my life?'

'That's an inductive leap,' I said, 'that I'm not sure I understand.'

'Fuck it,' Sarah said. 'I don't care if anybody understands.'

She began to cry and got up and went down the length of my loft and stood with her face pressed against the window, looking out and crying. After one hopeful glance, Rosie paid no attention to her, and continued to stare at the empty plate where the sweet scones had rested.

'I feel like a bad mother,' I said.

'If you were,' Brian said, 'you wouldn't be alone.'

50

Mrs Markham's face began to get gray as I talked with her.

'Of course, George was Sarah's father,' she said.

'No,' I said. 'DNA says he wasn't.'

'They could be wrong.'

'Not a good bet,' I said.

Her face got grayer.

'How do I know you're not lying to me?' she said.

'Why would I lie?'

'You've been trying to destroy me since I met you.'

I sighed and took a copy of the lab report from my purse and gave it to her.

'I can't read this,' she said.

'Take it to your doctor or your local hospital or to another DNA lab. The Andover cops can refer you.' I said. 'Or call the Boston cops. Brian Kelly is the investigating officer.'

'I can't do all of that,' she said.

'Any of that would be enough,' I said.

'I'm alone,' she said.

'You could choose to trust me,' I said. 'I'm not, in fact, trying to destroy you. I'm trying to help your daughter.'

'He's not her father?' Mrs Markham said.

She looked as if she was cold, or as if she was trying to be smaller.

'No, ma'am,' I said. 'He's not.'

'My God,' she said.

'So, would you know who her father is?' I said.

She wasn't looking at me. She was staring past me, staring at nothing. She shook her head.

'You don't know her father?'

She shook her head again.

'I don't mean to be indelicate, Mrs Markham, but if the father is not your husband, shouldn't you have some idea who else it might be?'

'She wasn't mine,' Mrs Markham said. 'She was George's.'

'Tell me about that,' I said.

'She was George's daughter from a previous marriage.'

'You told me she was born in 1982.'

Mrs Markham nodded.

'When were you and George married?' I said.

She looked at me without any sign that she understood the question.

'What did you say?'

'I asked when you and George were married,' I said.

'I don't remember exactly.'

'You were already married,' I said, 'when George was working in Moline in 1979.'

She did not speak.

'Which means Sarah was conceived while you and George were married.'

'She must have been born earlier,' Mrs Markham said.

'1978?'

'Yes. That must have been when.'

'Which would make her what? Twenty-six?'

'I guess so.'

'Mrs Markham,' I said. 'Sarah is not twenty-six.'

'I don't know what else to say. She is George's daughter from a previous marriage.'

'Except that she's not George's daughter.'

Mrs Markham put her gray face in her hands and began to cry.

'Who's the father, Mrs Markham?'

She shook her head.

'Were you so promiscuous,' I said, 'that you don't even know?'

'I was never promiscuous,' she said without taking her face from her hands.

'Then who was the father?'

'I don't know.'

'And you're not her mother?' I said.

'No.'

'Who is?'

She shook her head.

'Somebody is,' I said.

Mrs Markham shook her head again.

'How did she end up with you and your husband?'

Still bent forward, with her hands covering her face, she shook her head again. She began to rock.

'Mrs Markham,' I said. 'She had a father and mother.'

'Stop it,' she said. 'Stop it.'

She raised her face, the pallor parchment now, with two feverish red spots high on her cheeks. She began to pound on her thighs with her fists.

'Get out,' she said.

147

'Mrs Markham,' I said.

She pitched forward out of the chair onto the floor and lay on her side with her knees drawn up and continued to pound her thighs. Her eyes were clenched shut.

'Get out,' she screamed. 'Get out get out get out get out.'

I took the hint.

51

'He knows,' I said.

'Your father?' Dr Silverman said.

'Yes. He knows what my mother is, and he loves her anyway.'

Dr Silverman nodded.

'I always thought he didn't really love her,' I said. 'That he stayed with her because of the children.'

'He loved you more than he did your mother,' Dr Silverman said.

'Yes.'

The office was quiet. Dr Silverman was wearing a white cashmere sweater. Her hands were folded on the desk. Her nails were perfectly manicured. Her black hair was thick and shiny. Her makeup was amazing. Before I was through with therapy, I was going to have to ask her for suggestions. She seemed in no hurry. We could sit in silence for as long as we wanted to.

'Since I was a kid,' I said, 'I have had a recurrent fantasy. I am high in the mountains, in a pristine white wilderness, with a strong, quiet man. We are in a sort of shelter under an overhang. The snow is deep and new, with no tracks in it. It is perfectly still. Nothing moves. We are dressed in thick furs. The man has a Winchester rifle. A huge fire is blazing in front of the overhang. We are warm and very comfortable. There is somehow an infinite supply of food and firewood.'

Dr Silverman rocked slightly in her chair, nodding her head almost imperceptibly.

'How does that feel?' she said.

'In the fantasy, it seems perfect. Just me and the man together.'

'And the landscape?' Dr Silverman said.

'What?' I said.

'Talk about the landscape a little more,' Dr Silverman said.

'Very still,' I said. 'Deep snow, nothing moves.'

'And the rifle?'

'I don't know. When you're far out in the wilderness, a rifle is good, isn't it?'

'Does he use it to hunt?' Dr Silverman asked. 'Provide food?'

'I suppose, I don't know. It's not part of the fantasy.'

'What do you do, sitting there?' she said.

'Nothing. That's all the fantasy is, that image of us.'

'Do you know who the man is?'

'In the fantasy, I do,' I said. 'But you mean, really? Who he is in my real life. No, I don't know. Richie, I suppose.'

'Does Richie carry a gun?'

'Not usually. I've told you about his family.'

She nodded.

'You know many people who carry guns?'

'Yes.'

'Who was the first?'

'The first person I knew who carried a gun?'

'Yes.'

'My father, I... oh, Jesus Christ.'

Dr Silverman's eyes moved in the way she had that somehow prompted me.

'The gun,' I said.

Go ahead, the eyes said.

'The big gun.'

Dr Silverman nodded.

'Sometimes a gun is only a gun?' I said.

'Sometimes.'

'And sometimes it's phallic?'

She nodded.

'Sometimes it's both,' Dr Silverman said.

'So I'm in a cave in a mountain with a man with a big gun,' I said. 'All around is empty, frozen landscape with no life in it. And there's a big fire.'

Dr Silverman didn't say anything.

I smiled.

'Keep those home fires burning,' I said.

She kept looking at me without comment. Her eyes did their little move.

'What?' I said.

Go on, the eyes said.

'Home fires,' I said.

Dr Silverman's head nodded maybe a quarter of an inch.

'I'm keeping the home fires burning with my father and his big gun,' I said.

Dr Silverman nodded minutely.

'So why the dead-of-winter landscape?'

She moved her eyes. It was as if she had shrugged. How did she do that? I was quiet. She was quiet.

After a time she said, 'Dead of winter.'

'Dead of winter?'

'Your phrase,' Dr Silverman said.

'And in here there are no offhand comments,' I said.

She smiled and shifted in her chair in the way she did to indicate that time was up.

'Next time,' she said.

I stood and walked to the door. She walked with me, as she always did.

'Dead of winter,' I said.

She smiled and held the door open. I went out.

52

You spend your life never going to Moline, and all of a sudden you are there for the second time. I was at the bar in the cocktail lounge at the airport Holiday Inn and Convention Center, with

150

Millie McNeeley. I was having my first glass of white wine. Millie was drinking her third Manhattan, and chain-smoking Chesterfield Kings.

'I need you to remember,' I said to Millie. 'Two men are dead, two women are facing emotional destitution. It's not about discretion anymore.'

Millie listened to me. She nodded as I spoke. When I stopped, she sipped a bit more of her Manhattan, took another long pull on her cigarette, and watched the smoke drift up in front of her face as she exhaled with her lower lip pushed out. She didn't say anything. I waited. It was one of the things I had learned from my father about detective work. Silence pressures most people. Wait. Listen. Be quiet.

'That's too bad about George,' Millie said finally.

I nodded. Millie drank some more and smoked some more.

'He was a lot of fun,' she said.

I nodded. A small nod, just enough to cue her that I was listening. I knew where I had learned that.

'We had a little thing for a while,' Millie said.

Nod.

'He was married at the time.'

Millie finished her Manhattan and gestured to the bartender for another one and grinned at me.

'But I wasn't,' she said.

'When was this?' I said.

'Oh, lemme see.' The bartender brought her Manhattan. She drank some. I suppressed a shudder.

'It would have been right around 1979, 1980 – not too long after he got here. George was a ladies' man.'

'Though married,' I said.

'His wife was a poop,' Millie said.

'Were you his only, ah, conquest?'

'I wasn't conquested,' Millie said. 'I liked sex as much as he did. Still do, just harder to come by.'

'Were you the only woman in his life,' I said, 'other than his wife?'

Millie sipped her drink.

'Hell, no,' she said. 'George was hot. And the options in Moline aren't that great.'

'Who else was he with?'

'Every female at the station, I think.'

'Including Lolly Drake?'

'Absolutely,' Millie said.

For a moment, I felt like jumping off the bar stool and doing a little River Dance thing right there in the cocktail lounge. Instead, I remained calm.

'Were they a big item?' I said.

'No bigger than George and I,' Millie said. 'Remember, she wasn't Big-Deal Lolly then, just a kid with a call-in show in a small market.'

'Was George careful?' I said.

'About what?'

'Birth control?'

Millie laughed. It was a deep, smoke-cured whiskey-soaked laugh.

'George? George thought pregnancy was a woman's problem.'

'So he didn't use birth control?'

'No.'

'Did you get pregnant?' I asked.

'I thought it was a woman's problem, too,' Millie said.

'So you were careful.'

'I was.'

'How about Lolly Drake?'

'How would I know?' Millie said.

'You never saw her pregnant?'

'No,' she said. 'But I wouldn't have, anyway. She got the big syndication break on Heartland Media and moved on, and I never saw her again. I read about her sometimes. The way you do someone you knew once. I never heard about a kid.'

'Did she and George stay in touch?'

'Not that I know of. When she left, he moved right on to the new girl that replaced her... and I do mean onto.'

'Did she ever get pregnant?'

'Yes, but with a guy she married the next year. They got three more kids since.'

'Did you know anyone besides Lolly that George slept with who moved on shortly afterwards?'

Millie finished her Manhattan while she thought back.

'No,' she said, and gestured to the bartender.

'How long was George here after Lolly?'

'Oh, maybe a year. Then he said he got a big job back East and he left.'

'Ever hear from him again?'

'No.'

'While they lived here, did his wife fool around?'

Millie laughed the deep mahogany laugh again.

'Maybe with herself,' she said.

'She didn't have an affair.'

'God, no. I'm telling you. She was a prude. She showed no interest in any man I ever saw her with, and no man I know ever showed any interest in her. Including George.'

'Could they have adopted a child?' I said.

'Here? When I knew them? I doubt it. If they did, it was a big secret. Which is unlikely. The Quad Cities aren't that big,' Millie said. 'The local announcers are celebrities.'

'Are you a local celebrity?' I said.

'Hell, no, honey,' Millie said, and gestured at me with her fresh Manhattan. 'I'm a local drunk.'

53

After I returned to Boston, I took the Acela express train to New York, and Corsetti met me in Penn Station. He took my bag and swaggered ahead of me, plowing through the crowded station as if he and I were the only ones there. His car was parked up on the sidewalk by the entrance, with its blue light flashing. He popped the trunk, put my bag in, and closed the trunk. I noticed that he had a Kevlar vest in there and a pump shotgun.

'How'd you find her?' I said in the car.

'July's in the system,' Corsetti said. 'She got into it with a parking enforcement woman giving her a ticket. Whacked her with her purse. Got booked for assault on a law enforcement officer.'

'How'd the parking woman make out?' I said.

'She was built like me, grew up in Bed-Stuy. Was kicking July's ass by the time the local precinct guys arrived.'

'Surprised she didn't charge meter-maid brutality,' I said.

'She did, that's why they let her go. We won't bust your chops for the assault charge, you forget us on the excessive-force complaint.'

We were going down Seventh Avenue with the light still turning and the siren going.

'Is there an emergency?' I said.

'Naw,' Corsetti said, 'I hate poking along in traffic.'

'I gather July lives downtown?' I said.

'She lives in the Bronx,' Corsetti said, 'but there's less traffic in this direction.'

I smiled.

'Cute,' I said. 'Where in fact does she live, Eugene?'

'West Village,' Corsetti said. 'Twelfth Street.'

'Wherever will you park?' I said.

Corsetti glanced at me and smiled. When we got to the address, Corsetti slid his car up beside a two-zone sign on a corner near St. Vincent's Hospital. We got out. Corsetti swaggered, and I walked, west.

'I coulda reported to you on the phone,' Corsetti said.

'I wanted to be in on it,' I said.

'Y'all come,' Corsetti said.

We crossed Hudson Street against the traffic, with Corsetti stopping the cars by holding his badge up as we crossed.

'You ever get in trouble?' I said.

'For what?'

'You know,' I said. 'Using the siren when there's no need. Stopping traffic when there's no reason to.'

'Oh,' Corsetti said, 'yeah, I do.'

The address was a two-level brownstone-and-brick townhouse between Washington Street and the river. Corsetti rang the bell. In a moment, we heard a woman's voice over the intercom.

'Who is it?'

'Detective Eugene Corsetti, New York City Police.'

He put the emphasis on the first syllable of Eugene.

'What do you want?'

'Need to speak with you, ma'am.'

There was a security camera above the door. Corsetti took his badge out and held it up. After a moment, the door buzzed and Corsetti pushed it open. We were in a small foyer with a closed door in front of us and a stairway against the right wall. There was a woman at the top of the stairs.

'Up this way,' she said. 'We do things backwards here. The bedroom is downstairs, and the living room is up.'

We went up into a big, bright, many-windowed space that looked like it had been assaulted by a decorator. Into the early-nineteenth-century building someone had stuffed enough glass, stainless steel, white wood, abstract sculpture, and ivory wall-to-wall carpet, which looked dirty next to the white wood, to furnish the Trump Tower. In the jumble of styles, textures, tones, and shapes, there seemed no comfortable place to sit.

'Nice place you got here,' Corsetti said.

July herself was wearing shiny black capri leggings and a lavender DKNY sweatshirt that was much too big. She had a lot of curly blond hair, and very bright, glossy lips. On her left hand she wore a huge diamond with a matching wedding band. Her legs were skinny.

Corsetti nodded at me.

'Sunny Randall,' he said.

'How do you do?' July said.

'What did you wish to talk with me about?' July said.

'Could we sit down?' I said.

'Oh, sure, excuse me. Come sit in the kitchen. Would you like coffee? I have some all made. What is this about?'

We sat in her kitchen, which was right out of 1956.

'We haven't redone the kitchen yet,' she said as she poured us coffee. 'I'm sorry it looks so hideous.'

We sat on one-piece stainless-steel chairs with yellow plastic cushions.

'Very homey,' Corsetti said.

'So, what do you want to talk to me about?' July said.

The coffee was very good.

'You're a trustee of Bright Flower Charitable Foundation,' Corsetti said.

'Excuse me?' July said.

Corsetti said it again.

'I don't know what that is,' July said.

'Every month, you authorize a wire transfer from a bank in Gillette, Wyoming, to an account in Walford, Massachusetts,' Corsetti said.

'Wyoming?'

'Gillette, Wyoming,' Corsetti said. 'Wellington Bank.'

'I don't know what you're talking about,' she said. 'I never heard of the place in Wyoming, or the bank, or the place in Massachusetts. I don't know anything about Bright whatsis. I don't know what to say.'

Corsetti nodded. He took out a photocopy of a wire-transfer order and showed it to her.

'That your signature?' he said.

She studied it.

'No,' she said.

'Is Mr Fishbein at home?' Corsetti said.

'I use my birth name,' July said. 'My husband's name is Delk.'

'Delk?' I said.

'Yes.'

'Harvey Delk?' I said.

'Yes, do you know him?'

'Is he home right now, Ms Fishbein?' Corsetti said.

'No, he is at work. Do you know him?'

'When do you expect him?' Corsetti said.

'He's quite an important person,' she said. 'He's the manager of a very famous star.'

'Lolly Drake,' I said.

'Yes. You do know Harvey.'

I smiled.

'We've met.'

'When he comes home, I'll tell him. I'm sorry, what did you say your name was?'

'Randall,' I said. 'Sonya Randall.'

'How do you know him, Ms Randall?'

'We met casually a few days ago,' I said.

'You know,' July said. 'I'm not really comfortable talking with you like this. I think you should come back when my husband is home.'

'Which would be?'

'Oh, Lord, I don't know,' she said. 'He is so busy. He often works very late.'

Corsetti took out his card.

'Ask him to call me,' Corsetti said. 'We can set up an appointment.'

She took the card and didn't say anything.

'That signature look anything like yours?' Corsetti said.

'I'd really rather wait for my husband.'

'I got my wife's down pretty good,' Corsetti said. 'I been signing her name for years.'

July was quiet.

'Most people, been married awhile,' Corsetti said, 'probably do the same thing.'

July didn't answer.

'You think?' Corsetti said.

'I really don't know,' she said. 'I don't want to talk to you anymore. I will wait for my husband.'

'Loyalty's a good thing in a wife,' Corsetti said.

'Or a husband,' I said.

'People should care about each other,' Corsetti said. 'No husband's gonna sign his wife's name to something was gonna get her into trouble... is he?'

'Of course not,' I said. 'Harvey wouldn't do that, would he, Ms Fishbein?'

July didn't say anything. So, after giving her ample chance to do so, we stood and showed ourselves out.

54

Corsetti and I went like hell down to Hudson Street, the next afternoon, to meet with Harvey Delk in his lawyer's office, on the third floor of a big office building near Canal Street. We sat in a conference room opposite Delk and his wife, with a dandy view of the Holland Tunnel entrance. There was fresh fruit on a platter, and cookies, and a selection of sparkling waters.

Delk's lawyer was a smallish red-haired woman with bold eyes. Her name was Doris Katz.

'Coffee?' she said.

'You bet,' Corsetti said. 'Got to get my heart started.'

He smiled at her. She smiled back automatically. I could almost see her mind form the word 'jerk.' The rest of us all wanted coffee, too. Doris went to a side table, picked up the phone, spoke a few words, hung up, and sat down again. I admired the black wool suit she was wearing.

'It'll be in shortly,' she said. 'Now, just to be sure we're all on the same page, you are Detective Eugene Corsetti?'

'NYPD,' Corsetti said.

'May I look at your badge?'

'You bet,' Corsetti said, and produced it.

Doris examined it and handed it back.

'And you are?' she said to me.

'Sunny Randall,' I said. 'My real first name is Sonya, but I dislike it.'

'And you're a detective, too?'

'Private,' I said.

'Ah,' Doris said, 'I'm not sure we knew that.'

'Now you do,' I said, and smiled very sweetly.

'Do you have some identification, Ms Randall?'

I took my license from my purse and gave it to her. She

looked at it carefully and handed it back.

'Boston,' she said. 'Detective Corsetti, did you lead Ms Fishbein to believe that Ms Randall was a police officer?'

'Oh, no, ma'am. That's unethical.'

'But you didn't specifically identify her as a private detective?'

'Gee,' Corsetti said, 'I don't think so. We were just talking to Ms Fishbein. I mean, you know, have you actually told us you're a lawyer?'

I could see her mind begin to reexamine the word 'jerk.' A young man with long, wavy blond hair came in with a tray and passed out cups and spoons and napkins. He put a large coffee carafe on the table and a pitcher of milk and a bowl of sugar and sugar substitute. Doris poured coffee for us all.

When she finished, she said, 'We'll put Ms Randall's identity aside, for now, though should circumstance warrant, I can revisit it.'

Corsetti nodded eagerly.

'Sure,' he said.

'Is my client the object of a criminal investigation?' she said.

'Your client being Mr Delk?' Corsetti said.

Doris looked annoyed.

'Obviously,' she said.

'Not Ms Fishbein?' Corsetti said.

'Both are my clients,' Doris said. 'Are they under investigation?'

'Sure,' Corsetti said.

'Tell me about it,' Doris said.

'A series of wire transfers from a purported charitable organization were authorized with the signature "July Fishbein."'

'So?'

'The contributions figure in a murder investigation, and Ms Fishbein denies any knowledge of the transactions.'

'So?' Doris said. 'Why isn't that sufficient?'

'Well, Ms Fishbein is on the board of Bright Flower,' Corsetti said.

'I . . .' July started to speak.

159

Doris motioned for her to be quiet.

'Which seemed to come as a surprise to her,' Corsetti said. 'And which me and Sonya, here, found sorta puzzling, too.'

'How so?' Doris said.

Corsetti looked at me.

'Your turn,' he said.

'If Ms Fishbein is on the board and did authorize the wire transfers, then why is she lying about them?' I said. 'And if she's not on the board, and didn't authorize the wire transfers, then how did her name get on the board, and who did authorize the wire transfers?'

'You have support for this?' Doris said.

Corsetti took a manila folder out of his briefcase and slid it across the conference table to her. She studied the contents carefully. I drank some coffee. Corsetti stirred his noisily. I could tell that it irritated Doris Katz. She took a long time, reading everything. When she was through reading, she pushed the folder back across the table to Corsetti.

'Do you have a theory?' she said.

'Well, Sonya and I been thinking about it,' Corsetti said, 'and it seems to us likely that her husband used her name on the board of directors, and signed the wire transfers. Husbands and wives often have that kind of common-identity thing.'

'That's ridiculous,' Harvey said.

'Harvey, please,' Doris said.

She looked thoughtfully at both of us.

'Why would he do that?' she said.

'Because he works for Lolly Drake,' I said. 'And every time we go around a corner in this case, there she is.'

'Other than that sort of sequential coincidence,' Doris said, 'have you anything concrete to implicate either my clients or Ms Drake?'

'All the other women on the board of Bright Flower have husbands who work for Lolly Drake,' I said.

Doris paused for a moment. Then she said, 'My question stands. Is there anything that proves anything?'

'Not yet,' Corsetti said.

'Then I suggest you leave my clients alone.'

'A handwriting analysis might firm things up a little,' Corsetti said.

Harvey Delk glanced at Doris. Doris ignored him.

'Handwriting analysis is an inexact science,' Doris said.

'Except when it clears your client,' Corsetti said. 'We start pulling and tugging at this thing, and nothing good will come out of it for Mr Delk or Ms Fishbein or, for that matter, Lolly Drake.'

'My God,' Harvey Delk said. 'You can't…'

Doris cut him off with a hand gesture.

'Do you think either of my clients killed anyone?' Doris said.

'Jesus,' Harvey said.

'I doubt it,' Corsetti said.

'Then perhaps we have some room,' Doris said.

'Tell me,' Corsetti said.

'I'll discuss it with my clients,' Doris said, 'and get back to you.'

'Don't take too long,' Corsetti said. 'I don't want to have to come in and cuff him on the set.'

'We will be expeditious,' Doris said. 'And we won't be intimidated.'

'You might be,' Corsetti said.

55

Rosie and I were at our table in the corner at Spike's, waiting for my father. He was on time, as he always was. It was why I was early. Being on time was hard for me. I saw him shake hands with Spike when he came in. And Spike walked to my table with him. They didn't really understand each other, but neither of them felt a need to. They both cared about me, and I knew that seemed sufficient to them. When she saw my father, Rosie jumped up onto the table and wagged so hard I thought she'd fall off. My father picked her up and placed his nose against hers and gazed into her eyes.

'Never let anyone,' he said to her, 'tell you that you're just a dog.'

Then he put her back down and kissed me on the forehead and sat down. Spike brought us menus. My father ordered a veal cutlet with linguine. I ordered a tuna-salad sandwich. We both ordered iced tea.

'So, little Ms Gumshoe,' my father said. 'Whaddya got so far?'

I told him carefully – repetitiously, I was sure, but everything I could remember of every detail. He listened without a word, his elbows on the table, his thick hands clasped in front of him under his chin. When I was through, he ate some veal cutlet and a forkful of linguine. Rosie watched him carefully. She knew her chances of a forbidden table snack were better with him than with me.

'We both know the story,' he said after a time.

'You think?' I said.

'Sure. You still have to prove it. But you know that Markham had an affair with Lolly Drake about a year before Sarah was born. You know that Sarah is receiving money monthly from a charitable foundation apparently run by the wives of men who work for Lolly Drake. You know that Lolly Drake's lawyer hired some people to chase you off the case. You know that he got killed when you started looking into him. You know that when Markham finally did the DNA test, he was killed shortly thereafter.'

'But it showed he wasn't her father.'

'I suspect that was as much of a surprise to him as to anybody,' my father said.

'You think it's Lolly?'

'Of course it's Lolly. She got knocked up, she may not even have known who, but she told Markham it was him, for whatever her reasons, and he raised the kid. She sent money. Then, as things worked out, she became this moral standard-bearer of the airwaves, the apostle of love and loyalty, and it might have been harmful to her image to have abandoned her illegitimate child to a man not even her father.'

I nodded.

'Yes,' I said. 'That's what I think.'

'It's what any good cop would think,' my father said. 'How's this guy in New York, Corsetti?'

I smiled.

'I think he might be very good,' I said. 'You first meet him and he looks like some kind of thuggish city cop who spends his off time in the weight room, and he seems like a dope. Then you watch him talk to people for a while, and they all underestimate him, and you realize all of a sudden that he's found out a ton of stuff about them. He doesn't miss anything, and he doesn't forget anything.'

My father nodded.

'You think Corsetti knows?' my father said.

'What we know?'

'Yep.'

'I'm sure he does,' I said. 'But so far we haven't any proof, and Lolly Drake has a lot of resources. We can't just yank her in and sweat her.'

'You know what you're trying to prove,' my father said. 'You got a hitter to look for in both cities.'

'Might be the same guy,' I said. 'Same MO.'

'Either way, you got two cities to look for him in. You find him, or one of him, whichever, and you turn him and the whole thing clicks in.'

'And,' I said, 'we have Mrs Markham. She doesn't have a lot of resources.'

'Can the kid face up to her?' my father said.

'I don't know.'

'Might be interesting, if she can,' my father said. 'Get things stirred up, see what comes to the surface.'

'And,' I said, 'I can't believe that Harvey Delk can stand the heat.'

'Lotta guys like him don't,' my father said. 'Sharp guys, fixers, got a lotta power because they work for important people. Corsetti a tough guy?'

'Oh my goodness, yes,' I said.

'Then they run up against a tough cop who doesn't care who

they are, and all the savvy and secondhand clout dissolves and they're offering you their soul at bargain rates.'

'That sounds like Harvey,' I said. 'I'm not so sure about his lawyer.'

'Lot of lawyers for people like that have spent a lot of time closing deals from power positions – you know, do it our way or Lolly walks? It's been a while since they banged heads with a street cop who might put their client in the hoosegow.'

'Hoosegow?'

'You gonna be a cop, you ought to talk like one,' my father said.

'It's a funny case,' I said. 'I know who did it, and I know why, but there's no proof.'

'There is proof,' my father said. 'There's always proof.'

'I know.'

'You say Corsetti's a good cop. Brian Kelly's a good cop. You're an excellent cop. And there's too many people who got to keep too many secrets. You're gonna win this one.'

He cut a small wedge of cutlet off and gave it to Rosie. She took it carefully from the fork and ate it.

'Daddy,' I said. 'She's not supposed to eat like that from the table.'

'I know,' my father said. 'But I'm her grandfather. It's permitted.'

I smiled at him. 'Excellent?' I said.

'Yeah,' my father said. 'You're an excellent cop.'

He smiled.

'Pretty good daughter, too.'

'Even though I'm not married?'

'Even though,' he said.

'Mom seems to think it matters,' I said.

He gave Rosie another bite of cutlet, then grinned at me.

'Woman needs a man,' he said, 'like a fish needs a bicycle.'

'I know,' I said. 'That's what she always says. I would say she needs you.'

My father nodded.

'Em likes slogans,' he said.

'You seem so ill suited,' I said after a little silence. 'How have you stayed together so long?'

My father stared at me silently. Had I been a bad girl to ask? Then he smiled at me and patted my forearm.

'For God's sake, Sunny,' he said. 'We love each other.'

56

Sarah and I drove up Route 93 toward Andover. Rosie had assumed her spot, asleep between Sarah's feet on the floor near the heater.

'You can do this?' I said.

'Yes.'

She looked pale and tight, and she swallowed often and visibly. It was the way I had probably looked on my first day of school.

'You think this will be good for me?' she said.

'This is beginning to wind down, or up, depending on how you look at it. I think the bigger part you play in it, the more you'll feel as if you controlled your future, rather than things just happened to you.'

'You sound like my women's studies teacher.'

'Oh, God,' I said. 'I hope not.'

It was a bright day, but the landscape was gray and dirty where the snow had melted and acquired dirt and frozen and melted and acquired dirt and frozen. A few moments of lovely white followed by weeks of dirty gray. How metaphoric.

'You think she's not my mother?' Sarah said.

'We'll ask her,' I said.

'In some ways, it would be kind of a relief, you know? I mean, she was never very nice to me.'

I nodded. We went past the Academy and left down the hill and parked in front of the Markham house.

'I feel sick,' Sarah said.

'We're in this together, kiddo,' I said. 'We'll get through it.'

'I wish I hadn't started all this.'

'You are only asking a question you have the right to ask,' I said.

'I know,' she said. 'I wish I didn't.'

'Anyone would have,' I said.

She nodded and didn't say anything else. Rosie opened one eye as we got out, saw that she wasn't coming, and settled back with her heater. We walked to the house where Sarah had grown up.

When she let us in, Mrs Markham was wearing a flowered-housedress and sneakers. The house was silent, and felt closed.

Sarah said, 'Hi, Ma.'

Mrs Markham carefully closed the door behind us and locked it.

'So, you've decided I'm your mother again?' she said.

Sarah was silent for a moment.

Then she said, 'I don't know what else to call you.'

Mrs Markham didn't bother to invite us in. She simply turned and walked into the living room and sat on the couch with her knees together and her hands clasped on top of them. Sarah and I sat across from her. Mrs Markham's age and mousiness seemed to have increased dramatically.

'Are you my mother?' Sarah said.

'I've raised you your whole life,' Mrs Markham said without any affect.

'But did you conceive me, carry me to term, give birth to me?' Sarah said.

Mrs Markham looked at her for so long in silence that I thought she wasn't going to speak. Then she seemed to sag suddenly.

'No.'

'That's why you wouldn't take the tests.'

'George didn't take it so as to support me. He thought he was your father.'

'But he wasn't.'

'That's what them doctors say.'

'Do you know who my mother was?'

'George told me he got some girl in trouble,' Mrs Markham said heavily. 'He said he'd never strayed before and never would again. I knew he was lyin'. He strayed a lot. But he said the girl didn't want the baby, and would give us money to take it and raise it like it was ours.'

'And you agreed,' I said.

'Sure. We didn't have any money, and George wasn't going anywhere. So we agreed.'

'What was the deal?' I said.

'We move away before the baby's born and take her when she is born and never tell nobody, and we get money every month, for us and for her. It was a lot of money. I don't know how much it was. I don't even know how much she got. Nobody ever told me anything.'

'Did you resent it?' Sarah said.

'Was a good deal. Money was good. Until you started nosing around.'

'She resented it,' I said to Sarah, 'and she took it out on you.'

'Well, how was I supposed to feel, stuck with some whore's daughter? How was I supposed to feel?'

'And you never knew the woman?' I said.

'No. It was part of the deal.'

'Is this deal in writing?'

'No.'

'It was self-enforcing,' I said. 'If she didn't pay, you'd tell, and if you told, she wouldn't pay.'

'Except the bastard never even told me.'

'Secrets are safest when no one knows them,' I said.

'Now what am I going to do?' Mrs Markham said. 'They won't send any more money. What am I going to do?'

Sarah looked at her. There were tears on Sarah's face.

Finally, she said, 'You know, Mrs Markham, I don't really care.'

She stood up and walked out. I followed her.

57

Rosie had had her walk and her breakfast. I was drinking coffee and painting when Sarah woke up on the couch.

'You still painting that building?' she said.

'South Station,' I said.

'Why do you want to paint buildings and stuff?'

'I like how they look,' I said.

'If I was a painter, I'd want to paint flowers and lakes and stuff. Stuff that looked nice.'

I said, 'Um-hmm.'

Sarah sat up. Rosie came over and sniffed her ankle. Sarah patted her.

'I'm on my own,' Sarah said.

I stopped painting. 'You are?' I said.

'I don't have any parents. I don't have a boyfriend. I'm on my own.'

'You have me,' I said.

'I know. But it's not the same.'

'No,' I said. 'It isn't.'

'My tuition and room and board are paid for the rest of this semester,' Sarah said.

I nodded.

'I'm going back there.'

'To Taft?'

'Yes. I might as well get used to being on my own. I can't live on your couch forever. Pretty soon I'll have to get a job.'

'You could probably work for Spike,' I said.

'As what?'

'That would be up to him. Can you tend bar?'

'Not really.'

'You might learn,' I said. 'Do you have any money?'

'I have two quarters,' she said. 'But I can sleep and eat at the college.'

'I've got a hundred dollars you can have,' I said. 'When it's gone, maybe we can find some more. Just until you get on your feet.'

'I shouldn't.'

'You should. We're friends. Friends help each other out.'

Sarah laughed sadly. 'I hired you,' she said. 'And I can't even pay you anymore. And now you're paying me.'

'We're too far into this,' I said. 'I can't put it down. My accountant will find a way to deduct it.'

'Thank you.'

'You're welcome,' I said. 'When you're ready to go, I'll drive you.'

'You'll be glad to get rid of me.'

'I'll be glad to live just Rosie and me again,' I said. 'That's not the same thing as being glad to get rid of you.'

'Close enough,' Sarah said.

'No. Of course, I like to live my life as I am used to it. No one really loves a permanent houseguest on the couch. But I'm glad you had a place to come when you needed to, and if you need to again, the couch is still here.'

'Thank you. Do you like to live alone?'

'Yes and no,' I said.

'What's that mean?' Sarah said.

I smiled at her.

'Yes and no,' I said.

58

When Richie came to pick up Rosie, we were perfectly pleasant with each other. He sat on the couch and drank a cup of coffee. Rosie was beside him with her head on his lap.

'She's such a silent dog,' Richie said.

'She is often lost in thought,' I said.

'That would be my guess,' Richie said. 'She been okay?'

'Fine,' I said. 'How is your life going?'

'Fine,' he said. 'You?'

'Fine.'

'Does your wife mind Rosie?'

'No, not at all. She's not used to dogs, but she thinks Rosie is great.'

'And she's nice to her?'

'Sure,' Richie said. 'Love me, love my dog.'

'I hear a small reservation,' I said.

Richie smiled. 'She's not crazy about Rosie on the furniture in the living room,' he said. 'Or sleeping with us.'

'So what happens?'

'I prevail,' Richie said. 'Just like you would.'

'But what about when you're not there?'

'Rosie is always with me,' he said. 'I take her to work, everywhere. She's never alone with Kathryn.'

'But Kathryn's not mean to her?'

'Of course not. You saw Rosie with her. Rosie likes her. Kathryn's just not the same kind of dog person you and I are.'

The momentary sense of us-ness made me feel shaky. I didn't want to say it, I wished I hadn't said it. I hated it when I heard myself say it, but I opened my mouth and out it came: 'Do you love her like you loved me?'

Rosie was leaning on his thigh. He was resting one hand on her back. He sat silently for what seemed like a long time without moving, looking at me. Finally, he took in a lot of air, softly, through his nose.

'No,' he said.

'Do you still love me?'

Again, the long, motionless time. This time, he moved his hand enough to pat Rosie softly. She resettled herself slightly to take full advantage of the patting.

'Yes.'

I felt as if I could hear my own pulse. I listened to my own breathing. My computer was on at the other end of the room. I could hear it hum.

'I'm seeing a shrink,' I said.

'Good idea,' Richie said.

'She's very good,' I said.

'The best kind to see,' Richie said.

We looked at each other silently. Rosie wiggled over onto her back so that Richie could rub her stomach.

'I'm beginning to learn some things about myself.'

Richie nodded.

'I'm not exactly who I was,' I said.

'It's tough work,' Richie said. 'You should be proud of yourself for doing it.'

I nodded.

'Is there anything you need?' Richie said. 'The Burkes got resources, you know?'

'I never ever could quite be sure,' I said. 'Are you involved in the Burke family business?'

Richie smiled a little.

'I've told you no before.'

'I know.'

'So I won't again,' Richie said. 'Lemme tell you a story instead. When I graduated high school, my father and my uncle Felix took me out to dinner. My father said to me, "You know what we do?" and I said, "Yes." And my father said, "It's the life we chose, Felix and me." and I said, "I know." And my father said, "It ain't a very good life. I don't want you in it." Now you have to understand, my father probably said one hundred words to me in my first eighteen years. For him, this was like the Sermon on the Mount. "You unnerstand?" he said. "Yes," I said. "Awright," he said. "I want you to go to college, and when you get through, I'll be able to set you up in some legit part of the, ah, family enterprise." And being me, and being eighteen, I say, "If I want to." And my father looks at Felix and they both smile and my father says to me, "You do anything you want that's legal. Me and Felix can give you a head start, and I don't see no reason you shouldn't take it, but that's up to you."'

'And you never were in the rackets?' I said.

'No,' Richie said, and smiled. 'I went to college, and when I graduated, they gave me the saloon as a graduation present, and there hasn't been an illegal dollar spent there since I owned it.'

I didn't know what to say. I believed him. Why the hell hadn't

I always believed him? Richie grinned again, thinking back.

'Here's a nice touch, though. At this same dinner, my father also said to me, "Whatever you do, you're a Burke, and not everybody is going to be your friend. I want you to learn to shoot, and to use your fists."'

'And I said, "I already had a few fights in high school." And my father smiled at Felix again and said, "Yeah, sure. But Felix will teach you how to do it even better. Shooting, too."'

'And did he?' I said.

'Five afternoons a week for a year,' Richie said.

'And he knows a lot,' I said.

'Felix is getting older now, but he could still kill a man with a lollipop,' Richie said.

'And now you know how?'

'I do,' Richie said. 'It's not something you forget. And I practice.'

'But you don't use the skills?'

'Not yet,' Richie said. 'But since we're talking about this, Sunny, you gotta understand. I come from a family of gangsters and thugs, and I'm neither. On the other hand, I love my family. I will never turn away from them.'

'It's a fine line,' I said.

'It is,' Richie said. 'But it is a line.'

'Why didn't you ever tell me this before?'

'I thought when I said I wasn't in the business, you should have believed me.'

'You were right,' I said. 'I should have. Does your wife know this story?'

'No.'

'Has she met your father and Felix?'

'Just at the wedding,' Richie said. 'Neither was carrying a tommy gun.'

'So she doesn't know what I know?' I said.

'No.'

I was thrilled.

'So,' Richie said. 'You need anything?'

'A man named George Markham,' I said, 'was shot to death

172

last week in the parking lot in back of the Castle in Park Square.'

Richie nodded.

'Anything I could find out about that, including who did it, would be a great favor.'

Richie nodded again.

'I'll speak to Uncle Felix,' Richie said. 'Felix knows stuff.'

He put his coffee cup on the table and stood up. Rosie jumped down and went to the front door and wagged with her tongue out. I got her leash and gave it to Richie.

'When Rosie's with me,' Richie said, 'it's like she's with you.'

'Thank you,' I said.

'I love her like you do,' Richie said.

I nodded. Richie opened the door, and Rosie surged through it as far as the leash would let her, and stopped and stood motionless, waiting. Richie looked at me for a minute. Then, with Rosie's leash looped around his right wrist, he put his arms around me and hugged me. I was rigid for a moment, and then I hugged him back as hard as I could.

'Remember Yogi Berra?' Richie said.

My voice was muffled against his chest.

'It's never over until it's over,' I said.

'Something like that,' Richie said.

Then he patted me softly on the back, let go of me, went out the door with Rosie, and closed it behind him. I stood without moving, looking at the door, trying to get enough air.

59

The place felt empty when I woke up the next morning.

Rosie was with Richie. I felt a ripple of excitement when I thought of Richie. *It's never over until it's over.* I couldn't quite remember who Yogi Berra was. Some kind of sports person. But I knew the phrase by heart. I went for a run by myself, and came home and showered, and was drinking coffee in my bathrobe when the phone rang and I picked it up and Sarah's voice said, 'Sunny, you have to come here.'

'To your school?'

'Yes. My room. You remember where it is?'

'Yes. Are you in trouble?'

'No. There was a bunch of mail piled up while I was with you. I just looked at it this morning. There's a big manila envelope. It's from my father.'

'What's in it?'

'I don't know. I don't dare open it. I need you to come and open it with me.'

'I'll be there in an hour,' I said.

And I was. We sat in her single dorm room on either side of her small wooden desk in the small window alcove that gave her a view of the library steps. The envelope was on the desk between us.

'Where's Rosie?' Sarah said.

'With my ex-husband,' I said. 'We share custody.'

Sarah nodded. We were both looking at the envelope.

'Would you like to open it?' I said.

'No,' Sarah said. 'You.'

I nodded and picked it up. It was postmarked Andover, the day before he'd been shot. I took a nail file from my purse and used it to slit open the top. It had been through the mail system, and there were very few clues likely to be still clinging to it, but I tried to be careful anyway. In the envelope were four photographs and a letter. I put the photographs on the desk, faceup, so that Sarah could see them. They were full-frontal nude pictures of an attractive young woman looking coquettish. In one picture was a cute, slender young man with a camera who must have been taking the picture of them together in a full-length mirror. They appeared to have been taken in someone's living room. You could tell by the grain that they had been enlarged from snapshots. Sarah stared at the pictures without comment.

'Do you want me to read the letter to you?' I said.

She nodded, looking at the nude pictures.

"'Sarah Dear,'" I read. "'I have always thought you were my biological child, though I was not married to your biological mother. Recent DNA test results tell me I'm not. But in my heart, in my love, in my every fiber, I am your father and I love you as I always have. I don't know who your biological father is. Your biological mother is Lolly Drake. I've enclosed pictures, which I took of her, and one of her with me when we were intimate, to authenticate my case. I thought I had made her pregnant with you, and when she offered, I took you to raise as my own. I'm ashamed to say she paid us to do that. I don't know more than this yet, but I'm determined to find out. If things work out, you and I can talk about this letter and these pictures. The pictures are embarrassing; I was married. But it is all the evidence I have, and if anything happens, I want you to know the truth as far as I can tell it.

I love you, honey, Dad.

PS: I'll always be your Dad, whatever the DNA says.'"

I put the letter down in front of her. She didn't look at it. She was staring at the photographs.

'That's him,' she said. 'That's Daddy.'

'Yes,' I said.

'And that's my mother?'

'Yes.'

'Who did he say she was?'

'Her name is Lolly Drake.'

'Not the same one?'

'Yes. The queen of the airwaves,' I said.

'Lolly Drake is my mother?'

'It appears so.'

'Did you know?'

'There was a lot of reason to think so,' I said. 'Now we have proof.'

'What should we do?'

'First thing,' I said. 'I think you ought to meet her.'

'You'll be there?'

'I wouldn't miss it,' I said.

175

60

Corsetti, with his Yankees cap on backwards, swaggered into the Viand Coffee Shop uptown on Madison Avenue, and squeezed into the small booth opposite us. It was a fairly upscale area, but several customers must have thought cop as soon as they saw him. Corsetti knew who Sarah was, but I maintained the formalities and introduced them.

'How ya doin', kid?' Corsetti said. 'Whaddya got for me?'

Sarah looked at me. I nodded. She slid the manila envelope across the table to Corsetti. He waited while the waiter brought him coffee. Then he opened the envelope carefully and took out the contents and spread them out carefully. He looked at the pictures without expression. Then he read the letter without expression. Then he looked at the pictures again and read the letter again. When he was through, he put the pictures carefully back in the envelope and refolded the letter, and put it back. Then he sat back and drank some coffee. He put the mug back on the tabletop and looked at me and Sarah and smiled.

'Va... da... voom,' he said.

'It is Lolly Drake,' I said. 'The man in the picture is George Markham, who raised Sarah, thinking he was her father.'

'Yeah, you told me on the phone.'

'I want Sarah to meet her.'

'Won't get her convicted of anything yet, but sure, she can meet her,' Corsetti said.

'She's hard to get to,' I said.

'Remember, you are talking to a New York City police detective, and that police detective ain't just anyone. The detective is me. Eugene Corsetti. We want to see Lolly Drake, we see Lolly Drake.'

'Will we really?' Sarah said.

'Probably,' I said. 'Has there been any give in Harvey Delk's position?'

'You think you can get him to roll on Lolly?'

'Delk?' Corsetti said. 'Sure. Sooner or later, guys like Delk don't hold up. He'll rat somebody for us. Anything in Boston?'

'I have a, ah, friend, looking into the matter of George Markham's death.'

'A resourceful friend?' Corsetti said.

'Oh, my, yes,' I said.

Corsetti looked at Sarah.

'You know what I'm bettin', kid?' Corsetti said. 'I'm bettin' the resourceful friend is not actually a member of an officially designated police organization.'

He grinned at me. 'Am I right or wrong?' he said.

'You have good instincts, Eugene.'

He pointed a finger at Sarah with the thumb cocked, and winked at her and let the thumb drop as if to shoot.

'Good instincts,' he said.

At five o'clock, Sarah and I and Corsetti and his good instincts were all on the West Side, in the waiting room outside Lolly Drake's office, waiting for her to finish taping. Our arrival caused a flurry of lawyers, managers, flaks, and security people. The security guys in blue blazers and light gray slacks stood stolidly against the walls of the waiting room and looked fearsome. Corsetti, his badge clipped to his lapel, apparently didn't notice. Sarah was still carrying the manila envelope. She sat between me and Corsetti. I could hear her breathing. I could hear Corsetti, too. He was humming softly to himself, something that sounded like 'I'll Remember April.' At 5:20, a white-haired man with big horn-rims and a great tan opened the office door and stepped out between the security guards on either side of the door.

'Wow,' Corsetti said. 'Lewis Bender.'

The white-haired man stared at Corsetti.

'And you are?'

'Detective Second-Grade Eugene Corsetti.'

'Have we met?'

'Here and there,' Corsetti said, 'both of us being, so to speak, in the criminal-law business.'

'I represent Miss Drake,' Bender said.

Corsetti was having the time of his life. He was bouncing on his toes. I could tell he was hoping one of the security people would give him some grief.

'This is Sunny Randall,' he said to Bender. 'And this is Miss Drake's daughter, Sarah.'

Bender nodded his head gravely. It was almost a bow. The nod acknowledged that he'd heard Corsetti, but he had no opinion.

'Sarah's got a letter and some pictures she wants to show her mother.'

Bender smiled slightly. 'Wait here, please,' he said. 'I'll speak with Miss Drake.'

We all stood silently, Corsetti looking at the security guards, Sarah holding the manila envelope against her chest, her shoulder touching mine. She was very pale. Bender was gone probably five minutes. It was a long silence.

'Miss Drake will see Sarah alone,' Bender said.

Everything about Bender was pleasant and knowing and firm.

'No,' Sarah said. 'I won't go in without Sunny.'

'Are you a police officer, Miss Randall?'

'I am a private detective,' I said. 'Employed by Sarah.'

Bender nodded pleasantly. 'Excuse me,' he said, and went back into the royal chambers.

Another silence. Corsetti was tapping his fingers on his thighs in some sort of rhythm that only he could hear. He looked at Sarah and winked. More silence. Bender emerged.

'All right,' he said. 'Sarah and Miss Randall.'

'How do I feel?' Corsetti said.

'I don't believe it's personal, Detective,' Bender said.

He stood aside and we went in. He came in behind us and closed the door. Lolly Drake was sitting behind a large conference table. She didn't look at us when we came in.

'Lewis,' she said. 'I'd like you to step out as well.'

'I wouldn't advise that, Lolly.'

'Well, I don't work for you. You work for me. Step outside, please.'

178

Bender did his big neutral nod and went out.

Lolly said, without exactly looking at us, 'What have you to show me?'

Sarah looked at me. I nodded. Sarah took the letter and the four pictures out of the manila envelope, and placed the letter and the four pictures in front of Lolly. First, Lolly looked at the pictures. She looked carefully at each one for a moment, as if checking to see how she looked. She studied the one of her and George a little longer, and then, good heavens, she blushed. She put on a pair of silver half-rimmed reading glasses and read the letter. She kept looking at the letter for a while, long after she must have finished it.

Still looking at it, she said, 'What do you want?'

I waited. Sarah seemed to be having trouble getting her breath. Lolly looked up at me suddenly. She was getting it back together, the full-bore Lolly Drake charisma.

'What do you want?' she said to me.

'It's what Sarah wants,' I said.

Lolly kept her eyes on me.

'Well, what is it?'

'Perhaps if you looked at her,' I said.

Lolly hesitated and then, for the first time, looked at Sarah.

'Are you my mother?' Sarah said.

'Just because of this letter?' Lolly said.

'Pictures are suggestive. The guy in the second picture wrote the letter,' I said.

'All these pictures show is that I was young and stupid.' She looked at me again. 'About your age, I'd say.'

'Older,' I said, 'judging from the pictures.'

Lolly ignored it.

'So, what will it take to make this all go away?' she said. 'I have great resources.'

'We'd like you to provide a DNA sample.'

'Don't be silly. How much money do you want?'

'I want to know if you're my mother,' Sarah said.

'So you can walk around saying your name is Sarah Drake?' Lolly said.

'My name is Sarah Markham. My father was George Markham.'

'For Christ sake,' Lolly said. 'You don't know who your father is. I don't even know who your father is.'

The room was stone-silent. She had just admitted it, and I wasn't sure she even realized it yet.

'Mommie dearest,' I said.

61

We were all gathered now in Lolly's office: Lolly, Sarah, Lewis Bender, Corsetti, and me. The pictures of Lolly were discreetly back in their manila envelope.

'You realize,' Bender said, 'and I'm sure an ADA will so inform you, if it gets that far, that you have no real evidence of anything very much here.'

'The letter,' I said, 'and the photos would get us a courtordered DNA test, I'll bet.'

Bender shrugged.

'Surely all of this would be very embarrassing to Miss Drake,' he said. 'And possibly harmful to her career. But there is no evidence of criminal behavior.'

Corsetti bent forward with his forearms resting on the table and his chin resting on his forearms. He looked like a happy bulldog.

'We can let you fight that out with the prosecutor's office when the time comes,' he said. 'But here's what it looks like to me. Lolly starts out twentysomething years ago as some sort of weather girl in East' – Corsetti glanced at Sarah – 'ah, Overshoe.'

'I was a talk-show host in Moline,' Lolly said. Her voice was chilly.

'Sure thing,' Corsetti said. 'And if you'd stayed there, getting knocked up wouldn't have mattered. But you didn't stay there, and all of a sudden, getting knocked up became a pretty big deal, because you were selling some kind of true love and total feeling within the frame of marriage ragtime, and here you were, pregnant and single, and you didn't even know who the kid's father was.'

Bender looked bored. 'Are you through, Detective?'

'What I can't figure out is why you didn't abort her.' Corsetti said to Lolly.

I saw Sarah flinch a little. I put my hand on her shoulder. Bender raised his hand toward Lolly, but he was too late.

'I do not believe in abortion,' she said.

Bender's face showed nothing. 'Lolly,' he said. 'Silence is golden.'

She looked startled. It was probably a long time since anyone had admonished her.

'Whatever,' Corsetti said. 'All of a sudden you found yourself a whizbang, and you had to do something about the kid, so you conned Markham. I don't know if you conned him because you thought he'd be a good father...'

'He was,' Sarah said loudly.

Everyone in the room looked at her.

'I'm glad he was,' Corsetti said to Sarah, then looked back at Lolly. 'Or because he was easy to con and needed money. And the rest of the whole elaborate goddamned thing with Bright Flower, to hide the payments, and then threatening Sunny and the kid when they started looking into her parentage, then murdering a couple of people who knew too much.'

'Do I hear you accusing my client of murder?' Bender said. 'On no evidence at all?'

'Not yet,' Corsetti said. 'But there's evidence, and your gofer Delk will roll on you sooner or later. We got conspiracy. We got charity fraud, and we'll get murder.'

Bender shook his head as if Corsetti was mad.

'Lewis,' Lolly said. 'I want this to go away. I can set this child up with a trust fund that will make her secure for life, if that's what it takes.'

'Two people died,' I said. 'It's not going away.'

Lolly paid me no attention. 'You hear me, Lewis?' she said. 'I want this stopped now.'

Bender nodded thoughtfully. 'We'll talk again, I'm sure,' he said to Corsetti.

Corsetti nodded and stood. 'Only a matter of time,' he said.

Sarah and I stood with him. Corsetti paused a moment and grinned at Lolly. 'Nice photos,' he said.

62

I settled into my chair across from Dr Silverman. I had been seeing her long enough so that I now felt as if I was supposed to be there.

'I go back and forth to New York so much, I'm starting to feel like Amtrak,' I said.

Dr Silverman nodded. She was carefully dressed and made-up, but very understated. I wondered what she looked like when she was going out to dinner. If she let it go, she'd look like something.

'We have the case about Lolly Drake almost solved,' I said.

'Almost?'

'We know what happened – we can't quite prove everything yet.'

'But you expect to?' Dr Silverman said.

She was equally interested in everything I said. But somehow she never let me ramble. She concentrated entirely on me for the fifty minutes I was there. She saw every movement, heard every intonation.

'It's the old domino thing,' I said. 'We have a whole bunch of freestanding hypotheses. We need one hard fact to tip the whole thing. One person to say "I did it." Or "She did it." Or "They did it." Or whatever. It's like we have the fulcrum but we need a lever.'

Susan nodded.

'And Sarah?' she said.

'In a sense, we've solved her part. We know who her mother is, and we know that we will probably never know who her father is.'

'So that the questions she asked you to answer are answered or prove to be unanswerable.'

'Yes,' I said, 'except, what the hell is she supposed to do now?'

Dr Silverman tilted her head to the side a little.

'I mean, she's twenty-one, and with my help she discovered that she's alone.'

'And you feel responsible?'

'Not for finding out things. That's what I do. But... on the drive back from New York, I gave her a small lecture on it. She was responsible for herself. She needs to stop smoking, stop the drugs, stop sleeping around, stop drinking too much.'

Dr Silverman smiled.

'And was that effective?' she said.

'Of course not. She needs a shrink.'

'What you have done, which may be more effective, is to give her an image of competent adult womanhood, living alone.'

I smiled.

'And needing a shrink,' I said.

Dr Silverman acknowledged what I said with a small single nod.

'Would you see her if she wanted to come?' I said.

'Have her call me,' Dr Silverman said.

We were quiet. Dr Silverman seemed perfectly comfortable with quiet.

After a while, I said, 'I had a good talk with Richie the other day.'

'Really?' Dr Silverman said. 'What made it good?'

'He told me things about himself that he'd never told me when we were married.'

Dr Silverman nodded. She was leaning forward a little in her chair, resting her chin on her fist.

'He also said he still loved me... more than his wife... and he told me it's never over until it's over.'

'Do you think that solves your problems?'

'I... I don't... it made me feel thrilled and hopeful,' I said. 'But I suppose it's a little soon.'

She nodded very slightly, but I knew she thought it was a little soon, too.

'And there is the wife,' I said.

'And there is the wife,' Dr Silverman said. 'Do you think he's changed?'

'I don't know,' I said. 'But I think I have.'

'How so?' Dr Silverman said.

'Well,' I said, 'I had lunch again with my father.'

'Let's talk about that,' she said.

63

I was doing lunges up and down the length of my loft. Rosie kept a foot in front of me, looking at me over her shoulder, getting in the way, and having a nice time. The cordless phone rang. I picked it up and kept going and said, 'Hello.'

'Sunny,' a man said, 'this is Felix Burke.'

'Uncle Felix!' I said.

He was a pretty bad man but a pretty good uncle, and he kept his word. I kind of liked him.

'You got a cop you trust?' he said.

'Several,' I said.

'Well, bring one of them and meet me at Richie's place at two.'

'The saloon?'

'The saloon,' Felix said, and hung up.

Through the magic of cell-phone technology, I found Brian Kelly and he agreed to pick me up at 1:30. Then Rosie and I had a late breakfast. I took a shower and put on my makeup and got dressed. I noticed I was unusually careful about which clothes I wore. Brian and I had enjoyed an interlude shortly after Richie and I had parted. Things linger.

At 1:35, Rosie and I got into Brian's car outside my loft. I opened the passenger door, and Rosie jumped in and settled into the passenger seat. I had to pick her up and put her on my lap so that I could sit.

'I think it's against regulations to transport animals in a City of Boston police car,' Brian said.

'Unless they are exceptionally cute,' I said.

'That would cover all three of us,' Brian said.

Richie's place was down an alley off School Street, past the old City Hall. Brian parked the car, as illegally as was possible, up on the sidewalk past the Parker House. It was ten minutes before two.

'Let's sit,' I said. 'Felix likes things to go the way he said they should go.'

'There's a limit,' Brian said, 'to how much I care what Felix likes.'

'He's doing us the favor,' I said.

'Whatever it is,' Brian said.

We sat until two, then got out and walked across the street and into the saloon. Felix was sitting in the first booth on the left, across from a strong-looking young man with a square face and receding black hair, which he wore long on the sides and combed back straight. I knew Richie wouldn't be there. And he wasn't. Rosie dashed around behind the bar, looking for him. The bartender reached under the bar and came up with a long chew stick. Rosie sniffed it, and grabbed it, and joined Brian and me as we sat in the booth opposite Felix. Felix scratched her absently behind the ear.

'Brian Kelly,' I said. 'Felix Burke.'

'We've met,' Brian said.

'This is Tommy Noon,' Felix said. 'He's got some things to tell you.'

Noon looked at Felix. 'Off the record?'

'Tommy,' Felix said. 'You're on my record already.'

'We can listen off the record for now,' Brian said.

'I give you something, helps you out, maybe we can deal?'

'We might work something out,' Brian said.

'Guy comes up from New York, offers me ten to whack a guy named Markham?'

'You do it?' Brian said.

Tommy glanced at Felix and got nothing back.

'Yeah,' Tommy said.

'Who's the guy?'

'He didn't gimme his name.'

'How do you know he's from New York?' I said.

'He said so.'

'How'd he pay you?' Brian said.

'Cash, all hundreds.'

'Describe him,' I said.

'Kind of short, maybe five-eight, kinda fat, soft-looking. Big horn-rimmed glasses. Sort of fluty, you know, college guy, thinks he's important.'

Harvey Delk.

'Could you identify him if you saw him?' I said.

'Sure.'

'You know who this guy is?' Brian said to me.

I nodded.

'Can we get a picture?'

'Yes.'

'This helps you out?' Tommy said.

'Yes,' I said.

Tommy looked at Felix again.

'I get to bring a lawyer when we go on the record?' he said.

Felix made no comment.

'Sure,' Brian said. 'And we'll Miranda you, and your lawyer and the ADA can work out something. But first you got to pick your guy out of a photo spread.'

'You show me a picture of him,' Tommy said. 'I'll recognize it.'

'We can probably do all this tomorrow,' Brian said. 'You and your lawyer want to come in?'

Tommy continued to glance at Felix before he answered.

'Sure,' he said. 'Gimme a time and place.'

Rosie was working intensely on her chew stick. Felix looked down at her.

'What's she eating?' he said.

'That's called a bull stick,' I said.

'What part of the bull does that come from?' Felix said.

I said, 'Let's not go there, Felix.'

He studied the bull stick some more, and his face changed slightly. I realized he was smiling.

'And if you don't show?' Brian said.

'He'll show,' Felix said.

Brian nodded and watched Rosie chew her bull stick for a moment.

'Since we're off the record here, and just out of curiosity, how come you're so willing, Tommy?'

Felix answered. 'It's a way to avoid the death penalty.'

'We don't have a death penalty,' Brian said.

Felix shrugged. Brian studied him for a minute. Then he nodded and looked at me.

'Ah, yes,' he said.

64

Corsetti sent up some photos, and Tommy Noon picked Delk out every time. His lawyer was there; Brian read him his rights. An assistant DA named Missy O'Neil arrived, and she and Tommy's lawyer sat down to talk. I went home and called Corsetti.

'We got her,' I said.

'Your man ID'd Delk?'

'Every time,' I said.

'There's your wedge,' Corsetti said. 'Delk's got the *cojones* of a butterfly. He'll rat out his children. Lollipop will get a perp walk like the Bataan death march.'

We didn't have the cuffs on her yet. But I knew Corsetti was right. And I knew that Delk would babble like a spring brook.

'We've known for a while what happened. Now we'll be able to prove it.'

'And maybe get the guy who aced your lawyer friend,' Corsetti said. 'How'd you find this guy, anyway?'

'A favor from a friend,' I said. 'Next time I'm in New York, we'll have lunch and I'll tell you about it.'

'Will your witness hold?'

'He wouldn't dare not to,' I said.

'Because of your friend?'

'Yes.'

'Maybe you'll be down to testify at the trial,' he said.

'You think there'll be a trial?'

'No,' Corsetti said. 'Bender will deal. But we may need you down here, anyway.'

'I'll be happy to attend, Eugene,' I said. 'And if you're ever in Boston...'

'You can introduce me to your mystery friend,' Corsetti said.

'You'd make an interesting pair,' I said.

We hung up. Rosie was asleep on my bed, stretched out to the extent that her physique would allow. I walked over and lay down beside her and rested my hand on her hip. It was mid-afternoon. The sun was shining obliquely through my skylight, making a long, angular parallelogram of brightness against the end wall of my loft. Rosie was snoring pleasantly. *When either part of a relationship changes, she had said, the other part changes, too.* I heard myself laugh softly. My shrink had become 'she.' I had changed, or I was changing. I wasn't sure what I had been. And I wasn't sure what I was becoming. But I could feel the deconstruction and reconstruction process as if it were visceral. Maybe I was a good cop. All these years, my father stayed with my mother because they love each other. Who knew?

Without opening her eyes, Rosie shifted onto her back, with her short legs sticking up, so that my hand was now on her belly. I rubbed it gently. Actually, it was hard to say exactly who solved the Sarah Markham/Lolly Drake entanglement. I had found Moline and gone there – twice. I had slept with Peter Franklin in New York, although that maybe didn't strictly count as police work. Spike had helped. Brian Kelly. Corsetti. I smiled, thinking about Eugene Corsetti, accent on the first syllable of Eugene. He was a lot smarter than he let you know. My mind wandered. I stopped rubbing Rosie's stomach. She flopped her head around and looked at me with one beady, black eye. I began to rub it again. She closed her eye. And, of course, Uncle Felix. That was the big irony. Felix Burke found Tommy Noon and convinced him to confess. He was able to do both and make it stick because he was an amoral killer who valued family and kept his word. Felix was everything the law in theory opposes. Yet it was the simple fact that people feared him, and Tommy Noon was terrified of him, that made it happen. I knew he hadn't done it for me, though I knew, within his limited range, Felix liked me. He had done it because Richie asked him to. And Richie had done it for me.

The elongated sun square had moved up my wall. The loft had that kind of hissing silence that a home has, which is different from the silence in a forest. If Felix had killed somebody finding Tommy Noon, and I couldn't know that he didn't, would the gunshot make a sound? Was the saloon they had given Richie purchased with ill-gotten gain? Almost certainly. Did Richie run it honestly? Yes. Would we have nailed Lolly Drake without Felix's help? Maybe. It was all too complicated for me. Perhaps 'she' and I could talk about it. I shifted on the bed so I could hug Rosie.

'The times, they are a-changing,' I said to her.

Rosie seemed mildly annoyed at being woken.

Robert B. Parker's *CHEAP SHOT*
A Spenser Novel
Ace Atkins

The iconic, tough-but-tender Boston PI Spenser returns in an outstanding new addition to the New York Times-bestselling series from author Ace Atkins.

Kinjo Heywood is one of the New England Patriots' marquee players – a hard-nosed linebacker who's earned his reputation as one of the toughest guys in the league. When off-field violence repeatedly lands Heywood in the news, his slick agent hires Spenser to find the men who he says have been harassing his client.

Heywood's troubles seem to be tied to a nightclub shooting from two years earlier. But when Heywood's nine-year-old son, Akira, is kidnapped, ransom demands are given, and a winding trail through Boston's underworld begins, Spenser puts together his own all-star team of toughs. It will take both Hawk and Spenser's protégé, Zebulon Sixkill, to watch Spenser's back and return the child to the football star's sprawling Chestnut Hill mansion. A controversial decision from Heywood only ups the ante as the clock winds down on Akira's future.

Praise for ROBERT B. PARKER'S *CHEAP SHOT*

'Assured… Atkins's gift for mimicking the late Robert B. Parker could lead to a long run, to the delight of Spenser devotees' – *Publishers Weekly*
'Spenser is as tough and funny as ever, and Atkins has become a worthy successor' – *Booklist*

'*Cheap Shot* is the best yet, with a whip-crack plot, plenty of intriguing and despicable characters, and the lovable, relentless Spenser at its center… Atkins also has a deft way with Parker's style… Atkins is bringing his own energy and strengths to Parker's series. *Cheap Shot* is Spenser, by the book' – *Tampa Bay Times*

978-1-84344-449-7
£8.99

Robert B. Parker's *BLIND SPOT*
A Jesse Stone Mystery
Reed Farrel Coleman

It's been a long time since Jesse Stone left LA, and still longer since the tragic injury that ruined his chances for a major league baseball career. When Jesse is invited to a reunion of his old Triple-A team at a hip New York city hotel, he is forced to grapple with his memories and regrets over what might have been.

Jesse left more behind him than unresolved feelings about the play that ended his baseball career. The darkly sensuous Kayla, his former girlfriend and current wife of an old teammate is there in New York, too. As is Kayla's friend, Dee, an otherworldly beauty with secret regrets of her own. But Jesse's time at the reunion is cut short when, in Paradise, a young woman is found murdered and her boyfriend, a son of one of the town's most prominent families, is missing and presumed kidnapped.

Though seemingly coincidental, there is a connection between the reunion and the crimes back in Paradise. As Jesse, Molly, and Suit hunt for the killer and for the missing son, it becomes clear that one of Jesse's old team mates is intimately involved in the crimes. That there are deadly forces working below the surface and just beyond the edge of their vision. Sometimes, that's where the danger comes from, and where real evil lurks. Not out in the light – but in your blind spot.

Praise for ROBERT B. PARKER'S Jesse Stone series

'Coleman, best known for his Moe Prager series... successfully emulates the tone and style of the late Robert B. Parker's nine Jesse Stone novels' – *Publishers Weekly* on Robert B. Parker's *Blind Spot*

'Stone, who continues to struggle with his drinking and his obsession with his manipulative ex-wife, is the most engaging of Parker's post-Spenser contemporary protagonists... The dialogue is spot-on and the professional chemistry between Stone and his small force is its own reason to read the series' – *Booklist*

ISBN 978-1-84344-492-3
£8.99

Robert B. Parker (1932–2010) has long been acknowledged as the dean of American crime fiction. His novels featuring the wise-cracking, street-smart Boston private-eye Spenser earned him a devoted following and reams of critical acclaim, typified by R.W.B. Lewis' comment, 'We are witnessing one of the great series in the history of the American detective story' (*The New York Times Book Review*).

Born and raised in Massachusetts, Parker attended Colby College in Maine, served with the Army in Korea, and then completed a Ph.D. in English at Boston University. He married his wife Joan in 1956; they raised two sons, David and Daniel. Together the Parkers founded Pearl Productions, a Boston-based independent film company named after their short-haired pointer, Pearl, who has also been featured in many of Parker's novels.

Robert B. Parker died in 2010 at the age of 77.